The Real
American Dilemma

*New
Century
Books*

The Real American Dilemma

CsquareBO

Race, Immigration, and the Future of America

Edited by

Jared Taylor

New Century Foundation

First printing

New Century Books
Box 527
Oakton, Virginia, 22124-0527

Tel. (703) 716-0900
Fax. (703) 716-0932

www.amren.com

ISBN 0-9656383-0-8
Library of Congress Catalog Card Number: 98-65270

Cover design by Glenn Montecino

Manufactured in the United States of America

Contents

CRID

CR&O

Introduction

Jared Taylor

This volume takes its name from Gunnar Myrdal's hugely influential 1944 book, *An American Dilemma*. Funded by a grant from the Carnegie Foundation, it went through 25 printings–an astonishing record for a dense, 1,400-page work of sociology–before a second, "twentieth anniversary" edition was published in 1962. In 1966, Transaction Books brought out yet another anniversary edition (in two volumes) with a new introduction by Myrdal's daughter, Sissela Bok, who emphasized her father's commitment to changing human behavior by improving social institutions. No book, before or since, has ever had such an impact on how Americans think about race.

For Myrdal, the dilemma lay in the contradiction between unequal treatment of blacks and the sweeping statement about human equality in the Declaration of Independence. In an attempt to resolve this dilemma, the Swedish economist established what have come to be the ground rules for discussing race relations in America. He asserted that race is a trivial matter, that people of all races share equally in all abilities, and that if non-whites do not succeed in American society it is because of white racism and oppression. If the book can be said to contain a key passage, it is surely this:

> White prejudice and discrimination keep the Negro low in standards of living, health, education, manners and morals. This, in its turn, gives support to white prejudice. White prejudice and Negro standards thus mutually "cause" each other.[1]

America had a race problem because whites oppressed blacks and then pointed to the consequences of oppression as reasons to justify oppression.

In the half century since the publication of *An American Dilemma*, the United States has accorded Myrdal's analysis something close to sanctity. During the 1950s and 1960s, it enacted the entire civil rights program he had proposed. In 1965, Congress extended Myrdal's racial thinking to a new area by passing the Immigration and Nationality Act, which abolished national-origins quotas, and, for the first time, opened the United States to large numbers of newcomers from the Third World. If race was a trivial matter and an unacceptable basis for discrimination at home, it could hardly be defended as a criterion for immigration.

Since that time, large-scale immigration and racial integration–even forcible integration–have been defended in part because they promote "diversity." A mixture of races, religions, cultures, and even languages is now thought to be an inherently good thing for a country, and if large-scale immigration and high birthrates among non-whites reduce whites to minority status in a few decades, this will simply be the welcome result of having understood the benefits of diversity. A demographically renewed America will be the final triumph of Myrdal's view that race is a trivial matter.

The contributors to *The Real American Dilemma* believe that much of what Myrdal had to say was wrong, and that policies based on his analysis cannot work. Many of them believe that there has now been ample time to test these policies and that by even the most generous standard they have failed. It has been more than 30 years since the great triumphs of the civil rights era. Integration, anti-discrimination statutes, abolition of anti-miscegenation laws, and even affirmative action–of which Myrdal never dreamed–have not rung in the rosy future he and his colleagues predicted. American race relations are as tortured as ever. At the same time, concentrations of immigrants have brought perplexing social problems to Miami, Los Angeles, and much of Texas, and even the most optimistic boosters of "diversity" are hard pressed to describe exactly what the benefits are or are likely to be.

Many whites are not waiting to find out. They are moving away from areas with large numbers of non-white immigrants to those parts of the country where whites are still a majority. Their behavior suggests the belief that the new, polyglot America will not be an improvement over the old one, and shows their unwillingness to live in a neighborhood–or perhaps even a nation–in which they are a racial minority.

The persistence of racial friction and continued white flight are practical, empirical challenges to the assumptions about race upon which Myrdal based his analysis. Likewise, at the theoretical level, the past half century has seen enormous advances in our scientific understanding of race, and we know that much of what Myrdal took for granted was simply wrong.[2] And yet, the intellectual orthodoxy he helped establish remains as firmly entrenched as ever.

To be sure, there is an American dilemma. As Prof. Philippe Rushton points out in Chapter 1, there is a world-wide racial dilemma, but it does not take the form Myrdal described. Today, the American racial problem stems from a refusal to outgrow the narrow and unserviceable views that have failed to move the country forward. What passes for public discussion of the problem is a mechanical repetition of worn-out formulae that do not give solutions.

A different and more realistic view of race would include at least three elements. First, it would accept the evidence of our senses, and acknowledge that race is not a trivial matter. It has become fashionable to claim that race is an artificial social construct with no inherent meaning, but in the everyday thoughts and actions of millions of Americans it clearly means a great deal. In their choices of spouse, neighborhood, school, friends, and even hobbies and diversions, Americans commonly divide along racial lines.[*]

A second step in a realistic understanding of race is to grapple honestly with the question of racial differences. It is well established that blacks and Hispanics have higher rates of crime, illegitimacy, poverty, and even death rates from most diseases than whites. This is generally taken as decisive evidence that American society is "racist." At the same time, whites suffer from all these things at markedly higher rates than Asians but this is not taken to be evidence of anything at all. A realistic understanding of race must account for such apparent contradictions by accepting the possibility of biological as well as social factors.

There is now a vast body of evidence for an at least partially genetic explanation for group differences in ability and achievement. It is understandable that people should resist this view, with its unpleasant implications of genetic determinism. However, averting our eyes from the evidence has led to dangerous misdiagnoses. Since we have refused to accept even the possibility that the achievements of blacks and Hispanics (and, of course, Asians) are largely governed by differing levels of inherent ability, we have persisted in attributing low achievement among certain non-white groups to "racism" and "oppression."

Unfortunate attitudes and expectations may arise from this. For example, it is often proposed that our "racist" society teaches blacks, in particular, to "hate themselves," and that this causes self-destructive and anti-social behavior. In fact, shocking as it may sound, our society is inadvertently teaching blacks to hate whites. When blacks are told

---

[*] Professor Glayde Whitney's chapter in this book describes some of the misconceptions–and even outright dishonesty–of those who promote the view that race does not have a basis in human biology.

repeatedly that their problems are caused by racist white people–policemen, bankers, judges, politicians, bureaucrats, doctors, journalists, employers–the natural reaction is to hate them. If the United States has a problem of real, visceral racial hatred, it is not one of whites hating blacks, but of blacks hating whites.

This is evident not just in the fiery speeches of Louis Farrakhan, Al Sharpton, Sister Souljah, and Khalid Abdul Muhammed–which have no parallel in hostile statements by whites of anything like comparable stature. It is borne out in the cold statistics of inter-racial crime. When blacks commit violence they choose white victims more than half the time, which means there is more black-on-white crime than black-on-black. Violent white offenders choose black victims only 2.5 percent of the time. For every black mugged by a white, 24 whites are mugged by a black, and for every black woman raped by a white man, 200 white women are raped by black men.[3] On a per capita basis, blacks commit four to five times as many of what are officially classified as "hate" crimes as whites.[4] Statistics like these carry an alarming message: There may be violent consequences when society promotes hostility towards whites by insisting that "racism" is the cause of black failure.

The third element in a realistic understanding of race would be recognition that it is legitimate to resist demographic change. The shifting racial makeup of cities like Detroit, Los Angeles, Miami, East St. Louis and Washington, D.C. has profoundly affected the lives of their inhabitants. Much as we may be loathe to admit it, racial change produces social change. A largely Hispanic neighborhood is different from one that is largely white, black, or Asian, and it is perfectly natural that people who have grown up in a "white" environment should wish to live and rear their children in one. There is nothing sinister about the desire to preserve the distinctive character of one's environs or nation. Every people in every age has done this.

It is common to insist that racial diversity is inherently good, but if it were, Americans would practice it spontaneously. It would not require constant cheer-leading, bullying, and the heavy hand of government enforcement. Even if the problem is that white Americans are just too simple-minded to recognize the value of diversity, it is strangely authoritarian to force it on them. Even more perplexing is a goal of "diversity" and racial dilution for whites that no one seems to promote for non-whites. Policies must be consistent if they are to have validity and gain real support rather than lip service.

To summarize, a successful analysis must recognize that race matters, and that it may be impossible to build a society in which it can be made not to matter. Our challenge is to find workable, humane solutions based on a realistic understanding rather than on error or wishful thinking.

Breaking the Taboo

Sentiment to this effect is steadily growing, but it finds few opportunities for expression. This is because the Myrdal analysis has been an accepted part of the intellectual landscape for so long that many people consider it unassailable. Race is, in fact, the great taboo. There may be no other subject about which one can investigate the data, reach a conclusion, express it thoughtfully, and find oneself denounced not merely as mistaken but as morally suspect.

Conventional thinking about race has therefore become a little like a religion, complete with dogma and excommunication of free-thinkers. This obviously stifles debate. People know that certain views about race will prompt damaging accusations of "racism," so they keep their opinions to themselves.

The tragedy is that if there is any subject about which America needs the greatest possible candor and freedom of expression it is race. Race relations have always been the nation's greatest challenge, and are the backdrop to nearly every worrying front-page story about crime, illegitimacy, illiteracy, school failure, or welfare dependency. If we are not free to question current assumptions about race we will continue to blunder down a path that shows no sign of leading to a better future. In a liberal society, suppression of dissent of any kind is suspect; suppression of dissent on a subject of central national importance is a crisis that is, itself, an American dilemma.

This book is a volume of dissent. Its contributors have thought very carefully about the vital questions of our time and have reached conclusions that violate intellectual orthodoxy. All have, to some degree, paid a price for doing so; in Chapter 2, Samuel Francis describes some of the unpleasant consequences of dissent.

Every chapter of this book except the last is based on a presentation given at a conference on race and immigration held from May 25th through 27th, 1996, in Louisville, Kentucky. The conference was sponsored by *American Renaissance*, a monthly newsletter about racial matters, of which I am editor. A similar conference was held in Atlanta, Georgia, in 1994, and reactions to both have been perfect illustrations of how dissent is met.

The earlier conference included in its audience Dinesh D'Souza of the American Enterprise Institute, who was a subscriber to *American Renaissance*. He listened to the speakers and circulated through the crowd, quietly gathering material for a book, *The End of Racism*, which was published in 1995.

I happened to acquire a pre-publication copy of the book and was astonished to find that Mr. D'Souza had invented passages from speeches (which had been recorded), and had deliberately falsified "quotations" from *American Renaissance*. He appeared to be trying to make the conference sound like a gathering of potentially violent boors. I and some of the other speakers wrote to Mr. D'Souza's publisher. Books were already in print, but his distortions were so egregious that The Free Press took the extraordinary and costly step of destroying the entire first print run while Mr. D'Souza hurriedly made corrections. The text, as finally published, is still a caricature of the conference, but at least it no longer contains outright misquotations.

The End of Racism says many useful things about race; it repeats a great many arguments I made in *Paved With Good Intentions*, a book published three years earlier. Why, then, would Mr. D'Souza write dishonestly about the *American Renaissance* conference? He probably feared his book would be greeted with accusations of "racism"–which it was–and hoped to preempt them by saying, in effect, "Those guys are the racists: I'm a bold thinker." Let us assume that Mr. D'Souza stooped to falsification and charges of "racism" only because he knew his book veered dangerously close to forbidden territory, and because he was desperate to avoid excommunication. By doing to others what he was afraid might be done to him, he showed how well he understood the power of racial orthodoxy and how much he feared the wrath of those who guard that orthodoxy.

By 1996, *American Renaissance* was better known. When Louisville's guardians of orthodoxy learned that we planned to hold a conference in their town, they immediately set out to sabotage it. Activists first alerted the *Louisville Courier-Journal* to our plans, and the newspaper obliged with a long article about "white supremacists." The local leftist weekly went even further, with a cover photograph of a man in a suit wearing a Klan hood, and the headline, "Racists Without a Klu."

The *Courier-Journal* ran several more worried articles about the conference and denounced it in editorials not just once but twice. "Purveyors of racial division are, at heart, scared people," it observed, preferring to speculate about the mental state of dissenters rather than examine their views. The same editorial referred to a letter I had written to the editor as "a study in either semantic deception or self-delusion." The local television news was just as dismissive.

Activists visited the hotel where we planned to hold the conference, and put pressure on the general manager to cancel his contract with us. When he politely declined, demonstrators held "prayer vigils" in front of the hotel, asking God to interfere with our plans. Perhaps in the belief that God is more likely to answer prayers that are televised (or in the hope of bringing even greater pressure to bear on the hotel), they arranged for their vigils to be reported on the nightly news.

Two local high schools had planned proms at the same hotel on the same weekend. They were caught up in the hysteria about "white supremacy" and joined the chorus demanding that we be ejected. When the hotel once again said it would abide by its contract, the schools broke theirs. The proms had been planned for a completely different part of the hotel, ten floors away from the conference, and the students would not have even known we were there. What is more, one prom was scheduled for Friday night whereas the conference did not begin until Saturday night. Some ideas, it seems, are so loathsome they can contaminate an entire building, and do so 24 hours before the people who hold those views even arrive. It is hard to imagine a meeting on any other subject causing such a panic.

The conference itself was met with demonstrations, teach-ins, and more worried news coverage, none of which disrupted a marvelous series of lectures and discussions. Two of the speeches, mine and Samuel Francis,' were broadcast repeatedly by C-SPAN.

I suspect that the proceedings would have been a great disappointment to the demonstrators, who no doubt imagined all manner of fantastic goings-on. In fact, this moral ordeal for the city of Louisville amounted to nothing more than a few middle-aged men exchanging ideas–interesting and rarely articulated ideas, to be sure–but just a few men with ideas. We are pleased, in this volume, to offer these ideas to the judgment of the general public.

It should be unnecessary to have to explain what these ideas are not. However, as the press reaction in Louisville demonstrates, whenever debate strays from the guidelines, accusations of "white supremacy" are not long in following, so this charge may be worth a brief comment. First of all, "white supremacist" is probably the most pejorative, emotion-laden racial term that can be used against a white person. Because it is almost never defined, it is not usually a description of a way of thinking. Instead, it is a denunciation and is meant to intimidate and discredit.

Taken literally, the term "white supremacy" is presumably the belief that the white race is supreme–that it should dominate, rule or exploit other races. There is nothing in this volume or in *American Renaissance* that even remotely suggests this view.

White supremacy can be defined somewhat more mildly as a belief in the superiority of whites compared to other races. The consistent position taken at the conference and by people associated with *American Renaissance* is that the races are different, that these differences are reflected in society, and that they are a legitimate and necessary subject of study. Some differences are impossible to compare. There is no scale on which they can all be ranked so as to draw across-the-board conclusions about superiority or inferiority.

It is certainly true that the major racial groups appear to differ in average levels of a number of important traits like intelligence and resistance to disease. However, if whites are "superior" to blacks in this respect, Asians are "superior" to whites. Indeed, during the discussion after Prof. Rushton's lecture, one of the participants noted that if journalists were determined to call the conference supremacist they should call it "Asian supremacist."

The purpose of investigating racial differences is not to justify preconceptions but to better understand mankind. If, despite obvious overlap, there are racial differences in average abilities and predilections by all means let us study them. They are likely to have important implications for all multi-racial societies, and there has never been a time in history when ignorance was better than knowledge. Those who would suppress dissent and discourage inquiry by making irresponsible charges only reveal their own prejudices.

Today, as I write these words, we are approximately half-way through a year-long initiative on race sponsored by President Bill Clinton. He has appointed an advisory board to investigate the status of race relations, sponsored White House discussions on affirmative action and hate crimes, and held a semi-public "town meeting" during which a few citizens aired their views. The initiative is to produce a final report that is to be the basis for building–to use the initiative's full name–One America in the 21st Century.

The initiative is something of an irony. It recognizes that the presence in the United States of people of different races is a source of great tension. The initiative's name implies that racial diversity and the frictions to which it gives rise could even threaten national unity. And yet the President has repeatedly called racial diversity one of America's greatest strengths. Why does a "strength" require the sort of sustained national attention usually reserved for such things as drug addiction, AIDS, crime, or welfare dependency?

An additional irony is that this effort was initially billed as a frank dialogue that would grapple honestly with a difficult subject, but it has been anything but that. Even those who generally support the President on social issues have been disappointed by the initiative's timid approach. When, in November, 1997, the President's advisory panel announced that it would not listen to criticism of affirmative action, even the generally liberal American Jewish Congress protested:

"If the presidential panel wants to talk only to itself, fine," said AJC executive director Phil Baum, "but then don't pretend that it is a 'dialogue' and don't try to pass off its findings as a serious review of the possibilities."[5] It is becoming clear that the initiative will not venture beyond the clichés and emotional appeals that constitute conventional public discourse about race.

The President is to be congratulated for trying to do something about America's oldest and most agonizing problem, but his initiative is unlikely to accomplish anything. It will file its report and then be forgotten, just like scores of other commissions, outreach programs, and blue-ribbon panels. The reason is that the initiative refuses to question the narrow assumptions of the Myrdal analysis–that race is unimportant, and that once the prejudices of a few ignorant or ill-intentioned whites are overcome, America will be a land of racial harmony.

I believe this analysis has remained unassailable for so long because so many people find it attractive. It inaugurated a half century of hope, policy-making, and idealism, and for the majority of Americans it would be immensely painful to conclude that the ideas that launched the civil rights movement may have been wrong. It is very, very difficult to give up the assumptions that unleashed what has probably been the greatest peace-time outpouring of moral energy this nation has ever seen.

But as we look back on 50 years during which every major national institution supported policies based on the Myrdal analysis, it is high time to ask what we have achieved. Why is the present so unlike the future our leaders promised us? Where is the equality, good will and spontaneous integration the civil rights movement was to bring? What if the contributors to this book are right and Myrdal was wrong? Unless we are prepared to ask the *really* hard questions we will do no more than repeat the failed policies that have made the Presidential initiative necessary.

The transformation of the American legal and institutional framework that took place during the 1950s and 1960s was a remarkable achievement. It took courage to act on ideals and to work for what promised to be a better world. But it takes even more courage to admit that those ideals may have been false, that the goal was unattainable and perhaps not even desirable. Unless it can muster the courage to change course, our country has no choice but to sink ever deeper into the racial conflict and despair that has become the real American dilemma.

Oakton, Virginia, Jan. 17, 1998.

References

1. Gunnar Myrdal, *An American Dilemma* (2nd ed., New York: Harper & Row, 1962), p. 75.
2. See the chapters in this book by J. Philippe Rushton, Michael Levin, and Glayde Whitney.
3. U.S. Department of Justice, *Sourcebook of Criminal Justice Statistics 1991* (Washington, D.C.: U.S. Government Printing Office, 1992). See also "Crime and Race," *The American Enterprise*, May/June 1995, p. 18.
4. U.S. Department of Justice, *Hate Crime Statistics, 1990*, (Washington, D.C.: U.S. Government Printing Office, 1992).
5. PR Newswire, "AJCongress Criticizes President's Panel on Race for Refusing to Hear Arguments Critical of Affirmative Action," Nov. 24, 1997.

಄಄

CRISO

The American Dilemma in World Perspective

J. Philippe Rushton

In 1944, the Swedish economist Gunnar Myrdal wrote a momentous book on race relations called *An American Dilemma.*[1] In it, Myrdal blamed the underachievement of black people on prejudice and discrimination by white people. Political support for Myrdal's analysis swept away hereditarian hypotheses and helped outlaw segregation in the 1954 Supreme Court Decision of *Brown v Board of Education.* Myrdal's ideas also fueled the 1964 Civil Rights Act leading to school busing and affirmative action and to the War on Poverty, including Head Start programs. Whatever benefits may have resulted from this transformation of American society, blacks and whites were not equalized in IQ scores.

In this chapter, I will show that equalizing environments cannot, in fact, remove black/white disparities in IQ because these are substantially genetic in origin. Indeed, my thesis is that racial differences go well beyond what is typically considered. First, the differences go beyond blacks and whites to define a 3-way gradient from Orientals to whites to blacks. Second, the differences go beyond IQ scores to include brain size, reproductive physiology, personality and temperament, crime, speed of physical maturation, and longevity (see Table 1, following page). Third, the differences go beyond the United States and are found internationally. Fourth, the differences go beyond environmental causation and are deeply rooted in gene-based evolutionary processes.

Although the historical record shows an African cultural disadvantage has existed, relative to Europeans and Asians, ever since Europeans first made contact over 2,000 years ago, it was possible to argue, until recently, that "reasonable doubt" existed about the genetic basis of black/white differences. Today, however, the evidence overwhelmingly favors the view that genes are required to explain the data. Surveys of experts in psychological testing and behavioral genetics show that

Relative Ranking on Diverse Variables

	Orientals	Whites	Blacks
Brain Size			
Autopsy data (cm³ equiv.)	1,351	1,356	1,223
Endocranial volume (cm³)	1,415	1,362	1,268
Head measures (cm³)	1,356	1,329	1,294
Cortical neurons (billions)	13.767	13.665	13.185
Intelligence			
IQ test scores	106	100	85
Decision times	Faster	Intermediate	Slower
Cultural achievements	Higher	Higher	Lower
Maturation Rate			
Gestation time	?	Intermediate	Earlier
Skeletal development	Later	Intermediate	Earlier
Motor development	Later	Intermediate	Earlier
Dental development	Later	Intermediate	Earlier
Age of first intercourse	Later	Intermediate	Earlier
Age of first pregnancy	Later	Intermediate	Earlier
Life-span	Longer	Intermediate	Shorter
Personality			
Activity	Lower	Intermediate	Higher
Aggressiveness	Lower	Intermediate	Higher
Cautiousness	Higher	Intermediate	Lower
Dominance	Lower	Intermediate	Higher
Impulsiveness	Lower	Intermediate	Higher
Self-concept	Lower	Intermediate	Higher
Sociability	Lower	Intermediate	Higher
Social Organization			
Marital stability	Higher	Intermediate	Lower
Law abidingness	Higher	Intermediate	Lower
Mental health	Higher	Intermediate	Lower
Administrative capacity	Higher	Higher	Lower
Reproductive Effort			
Two-egg twins/1,000 births	4	8	16
Hormone levels	Lower	Intermediate	Higher
Sexual characteristics	Smaller	Intermediate	Larger
Intercourse frequencies	Lower	Intermediate	Higher
Permissive attitudes	Lower	Intermediate	Higher
Sexually transmitted diseases	Lower	Intermediate	Higher

most judge the race differences in IQ to be genetic in origin.[3,4]

The Bell Curve

If Myrdal's 1944 book heralded an intellectual revolution, then Richard Herrnstein and Charles Murray's *The Bell Curve*[5] signaled the counter-revolution. This penetrating analysis of social mobility reported the results of a 12-year longitudinal study of 11,878 youths (3,022 of whom were African-American). Most 17-year-olds with high scores on the Armed Forces Qualification Test (black as well as white) went on to occupational success by their late 20s and early 30s whereas many of those with low scores went on to welfare dependency. *The Bell Curve* made it to the *New York Times* Bestsellers' List for 14 weeks, selling over 400,000 copies and spawning several anthologies of commentary.[6,7]

The predictive power of IQ scores had long been known by those familiar with the technical literature and interested in individual differences.[8,9] But in the world of policy makers and pundits, *The Bell Curve* was a blockbuster, potentially altering the way they viewed the world, a fact not lost on its critics. *The Bell Curve* confirmed a genetic model of social stratification and, as such, improved on exclusively sociocultural and economic models. Blacks with IQs of 117, even those from disrupted ghetto families, were more likely to enter a profession than were whites with IQs of 100, even those from intact suburban families. Indeed, blacks with an IQ of 117 were twice as likely to enter a profession as were whites with an IQ of 117, presumably an effect of the affirmative action quota system.

Almost all commentators have accepted that the bell curve of IQ distribution for "African" Americans is offset lower than the ones for "Latino," "white," "Asian," and "Jewish" Americans. (In *The Bell Curve* these IQ equivalents were 85, 89, 103, 106, and 115, respectively, pp. 273-278). The flashpoint of discussion, however, centered on whether the black/white difference is partly genetic. *The Bell Curve* presented a clear rendition of the usual syllogism, that (a) IQ test scores are heritable in both white and black populations, (b) white IQs are higher than black IQs, so (c) probabilistically, the white/black IQ difference is partly heritable.

The Bell Curve brought to attention Richard Lynn's compilation of the international data on IQ showing that Orientals (people of Chinese, Japanese, and Korean descent) score higher on tests of mental ability than do whites, both within the U.S.A. and in Asia, whereas Africans and Caribbeans score lower.[10,11] Lynn showed that Orientals in East Asia and North America typically have average IQs in the range of 101 to 111. Whites in Europe, South Africa, Australasia, and North America typically have average IQs of from 85 to 115 with an overall mean of 100. Blacks living south of the Sahara, in the Caribbean, in Britain, and in North America typically have IQs of from 70 to 90.

Especially noteworthy has been Lynn's calculation of an IQ of only 70 for Africans south of the Sahara. Many reviewers expressed strong disbelief about such a low IQ, holding it impossible that, by European standards, 50 percent of black Africa is "mentally retarded."[12,13] But an African IQ of 70 has been confirmed in three studies since Lynn's 1991 review, each of which used Raven's Progressive Matrices, a test usually regarded as an excellent measure of the non-verbal component of general intelligence and one not bound by culturally specific information. First, Kenneth Owen found a black African IQ of 70 in a sample of over 1,000 South African 13-year-olds.[14] Second, Fred Zindi, a black Zimbabwean, found an African IQ of 70 in a study that matched 204 12- to 14-year-old Zimbabwean students and 202 English students for sex, educational level, and "working class" background.[15] Third, Richard Lynn found an African IQ of 70 in a study of Ethiopian immigrants to Israel.[16]

Of course, questions can be raised about the validity of using tests for racial comparisons. However, because the tests show similar patterns of internal item consistency and predictive validity for all groups and because the same differences are found on relatively culture-free tests, most psychometricians think that the tests are valid measures of racial differences.[2,3,9] This was also the judgment of a recent Task Force Report from the American Psychological Association.[17]

Speed of decision making (reaction time) in 9- to 12-year-olds shows the same three-way racial pattern as do test scores. Children were asked to decide which of several lights was on or stood out from others and move a hand to press a button. All of the children could perform the task in less than one second, but children with higher IQs performed it faster than those with lower scores. Richard Lynn found that Oriental children from Hong Kong and Japan were faster in reaction time (controlling for movement time) than were white children from Britain and Ireland, who in turn were faster than black children from South Africa.[10,18] Arthur Jensen found this same pattern of racial differences in California.[19,20]

Racial Differences in Brain Size

A small but robust relation has been firmly established between IQ scores and brain size.[21] This relationship has been most clearly shown using Magnetic Resonance Imaging (MRI) which creates, *in vivo*, a three dimensional image of the brain. The strength of the relationship between brain size and IQ (r = 0.40) is roughly equivalent to the strength of the relationship between social class and IQ. Lower correlations can be found between head circumference measures and IQ. The correlation here is about 0.20 but the relationship is robust, having been found for many different ages and in many different populations.

The results from numerous modern studies converge on the conclusion that the brains of Orientals and their descendants average about 17 cm³ (1 in³) larger than those of Europeans and their descendants, whose brains average about 80 cm³ (5 in³) larger than those of Africans and their descendants.[2,21] This racial gradient has been independently established using three procedures: (a) wet brain weight at autopsy, (b) volume of empty skulls using filler, and (c) volume estimated from external head sizes. Recently, (d) a MRI study has confirmed the white/black difference.

Consider just a few of the recently conducted studies, some from the U.S. and others from around the world, showing again the universality of the racial pattern. Dr. Khang-Cheng Ho and his associates at the Medical College of Wisconsin reported autopsy brain weights on 1,261 individuals. Holding constant age, sex, and body size, they found that white Americans averaged a brain weight of 1,323 grams whereas black Americans averaged 1,223 grams.[22] Kenneth Beals and his colleagues in anthropology examined endocranial volume in up to 20,000 skulls from around the world and found that East Asians, Europeans, and Africans averaged cranial volumes of 1,415, 1,362, and 1,268 cm³ respectively.[23] A study by me using head measurements, from a stratified random sample of 6,325 U.S. Army personnel, found that Orientals, whites, and blacks in the U.S. Army averaged 1,416, 1,380, and 1,359 cm³, respectively.[24] Another study by me using head sizes, this time from tens of thousands of men and women collated by the International Labour Office from around the world, found that Asians, Europeans, and Africans averaged 1,308, 1,297, and 1,241 cm³, respectively.[25] Finally, a study in Britain used MRI and found Africans and Caribbeans averaged a smaller brain volume than did British whites.[26]

Racial differences in brain size show up early in life. Data from the National Collaborative Perinatal Project on 19,000 black children and 17,000 white children show that black children have a smaller head circumference at birth and, although black children are born shorter in stature and lighter in weight than white children, by age 7 "catch-up growth" leads black children to be larger in body size than white children but still smaller in head circumference.[27] In this study, head circumference at birth was found to correlate with IQ at age 7 in both black and white children.

Crime

Although it may be little more than a cliché to point out that blacks in the U.S. commit more crimes of violence than do whites or Asians, it is seldom realized just how strong the race/crime relation is. Figures 1 and 2 (see following pages) are taken from Glayde Whitney's 1995 presidential address to the Behavior Genetics Association. Figure 1 shows the homicide rate per 100,000 of population plotted against the percentage of the population that is black for the 50 states of the United States.[28] The correlation is +0.77. Figure 2 shows the relation again between number of black people in the state and homicide rate, this time with the addition of data for Washington, D.C. in the upper right of the figure. The very high murder rate for Washington, D.C., which is over 70 percent black, is simply what one would predict, given knowledge of its population composition.

It is seldom officially noted that Orientals are *underrepresented* in U.S. crime statistics relative to whites and have been ever since record-keeping began. In the 1920s, the underrepresentation of Orientals in crime was seen as providing a theoretical problem for criminologists who solved the problem using the concept of the "ghetto." For Orientals, a ghetto was seen as a place that protected members from the disruptive tendencies of the outside society. Among blacks, however, the ghetto was said to foster crime and to have done so since at least the turn of the century. The U.S. census of 1910 showed more blacks than whites in jail, in the North as well as the South. Official figures from the 1930s through the 1950s showed blacks were arrested for crimes of violence in ratios to whites of from 6:1 to 16:1.[29]

A government Commission in Ontario recently reported that, in Canada too, blacks were five times more likely to be in jail than were whites and ten times more likely than were Orientals.[30] Politically correct, the Commission argued that the disproportion was due to systemic

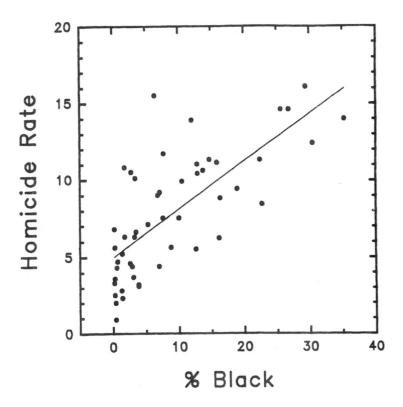

Figure 1. Homicide rate per 100,000 population, plotted against percent of the population that is black, for the 50 states. The homicide data are from the U.S. Department of Justice (1981), while the population percentages are from the 1980 census. The correlation is r = +0.77. From Glayde Whitney (ref. 28, fig. 4). © 1995 by The Institute for the Study of Man. Reprinted with permission.

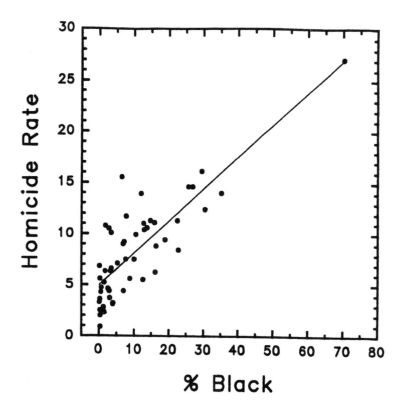

Figure 2. Homicide rate per 100,000 population, plotted against per-cent of the population that is black, for the 50 states, as in Figure 1, with the addition of data for Washington, D.C. in the upper right of the figure. From Glayde Whitney (ref. 28, fig. 5). © 1995 by The Institute for the Study of Man. Reprinted with permission.

anti-black racism operating throughout the Ontario criminal justice system (it ignored the Oriental underrepresentation). In England, too, results over the last 15 years show that although blacks constitute only about 10 percent of the population of London, they commit about 50 percent of the violent crime.

The global nature of the racial pattern of violent crime is readily confirmed using INTERPOL yearbooks, published by the international police organization. Analyses of these yearbooks throughout the 1980s showed that African and Caribbean countries had double the rate of violent crime than did European countries and three times that of countries in the Pacific Rim. For example, averaging over the three crimes of murder, rape, and serious assault for 1984 and 1986 showed that the figures per 100,000 population were, respectively, 142, 74, and 43.[31] Subsequently, an analysis of the data for 1989-90 again found the rates of murder, rape, and serious assault were three times higher for African and Caribbean countries than for Pacific Rim countries, with European countries once again intermediate.[32] For 1989-90, the rates of violent crime per 100,000 population for Africans, Europeans, and Asians were 240, 75, and 32.

Family Structure, Testosterone, and Personality

Learning to follow rules is traditionally thought to depend on family socialization. Since the 1965 Moynihan Report documented the high rates of marital dissolution, frequent heading of families by women, and numerous illegitimate births, the figures cited as evidence for the instability of the black family in America have tripled.[2] A similarly constituted matrifocal black family is found in the Caribbean, with father-absent households and a lack of paternal certainty. Moreover, there is separate bookkeeping by co-habitants; even when blacks are married, the tendency is not to pool resources, implying a readiness to part company. The Caribbean pattern, like the American one, is typically attributed to the long legacy of slavery. The slavery hypothesis, however, does not fit data from sub-Saharan Africa. Reviewing long-standing African marriage systems in the 1989 issue of *Ethology and Sociobiology*,[33] Patricia Draper of Pennsylvania State University summarized: "coupled with low investment parenting is a mating pattern that permits early sexual activity, loose economic and emotional ties between spouses . . . and in many cases the expectation on the part of both spouses that the marriage will end in divorce or separation, followed by the formation of another union."

The African marriage system may depend partly on hormonally based traits of personality. Biological variables such as the sex hormone testosterone are implicated in the tendency toward multiple relationships as well as to commit crime. One study, published in the 1993 issue of *Criminology*, showed clear evidence of a testosterone-crime link based on an analysis of 4,462 U.S. military personnel.[34] Other studies have linked testosterone to an aggressive and impulsive temperament and also to sexual behavior. Testosterone levels help to explain why young men are disproportionately represented in crime statistics relative to young women, and why younger people are more trouble-prone than older people. Testosterone reliably differentiates the sexes and is known to decline with age.

Race differences exist in average testosterone levels. Studies show three to 19 percent more testosterone in black college students and military veterans than in their white counterparts.[35] Studies among the Japanese show a correspondingly lower amount of testosterone than among white Americans. Some investigations were carried out by medical researchers interested in cancer of the prostate, one determinant of which is testosterone. Black men have higher rates of prostate cancer than white men, who in turn have higher rates than Oriental men.[36]

Hormones may also influence personality and temperament. International data show that blacks are more talkative, less restrained and more excitable than whites. Whites in turn are more talkative, less restrained and more excitable than Orientals. With infants and young children, observer ratings are the main method employed, whereas with adults the use of standardized tests are more frequent.[2] One study in French-speaking Québec examined 825 4- to 6-year-olds from 66 countries rated by 50 teachers. All the children were in preschool French-language immersion classes for immigrant children. Teachers consistently reported better social adjustment and less hostility-aggression from East Asian than from white than from African-Caribbean children.[37] Another study based on 25 countries from around the world showed that East Asians were less extroverted and more anxiety-prone than Europeans, who in turn were less outgoing and more restrained than Africans.[38]

Speed of Maturation

In the United States, black mothers have long been known to have a shorter gestation period than white mothers. By week 39, 51 percent of black children have been born, whereas the figure for white children is 33 percent.[36,39] Similar results have been observed in Europe, where women of European ancestry have been compared with women of African ancestry.[40] Other observations reveal that, although black babies are born earlier, they are physiologically more mature than white babies, as measured by pulmonary function and amniotic fluid.

Black precocity in physical maturation continues through life. On well-standardized tests, scores indicate that black babies from Africa, the Caribbean, and the United States mature faster than white babies on measures taken from birth to 12 months in coordination and head lifting, in muscular strength and turning over, and in locomotion; at 15 to 20 months, black babies are more advanced in the ability to put on clothing.[41,42] In contrast, on well-standardized measures, Asian children are more delayed than white children. Asian children typically do not walk until 13 months, compared with 12 months for white children and 11 months for black children.[43] Regarding dental development, African samples begin the first phase of permanent tooth eruption at age 5.8 years and finish at 7.6 years; Caucasoids begin at 6.1 years and finish at 7.7 years; and Mongoloids begin at 6.1 years and finish at 7.8 years.[2]

Behavioral life-cycle traits show a similar set of differences among the three populations. These include age at first intercourse and age at first pregnancy, as well as longevity. For example, at all ages, blacks have higher mortality rates from numerous causes than whites in the United States, and the gap has widened over the last 30 years.[36] Asians have lower mortality rates than whites.

Rate of Ovulation, Sexuality, and AIDS

Sex hormones also influence reproductive physiology. Whereas the average woman produces one egg every 28 days in the middle of the menstrual cycle, some women have shorter cycles and others produce more than one egg, both events that translate into greater fecundity including the birth of dizygotic (two-egg) twins.[2] Black women average shorter menstrual cycles than white women and produce a greater frequency of dizygotic twins. The rate per 1,000 births is fewer than four among East Asians, eight among whites, and 16 or more among Africans and African-Americans.[44]

Racial differences exist in sexual behavior, as documented by numerous surveys including some carried out by the World Health Organization.[2] Africans, African-Americans and blacks living in Britain are more sexually active, at an earlier age, and with more sexual partners than are Europeans and white Americans, who in turn are more sexually active, at an earlier age, and with more sexual partners than are Asians, Asian-Americans, and Asians living in Britain. Sexual behavior translates into consequences, including pregnancies and sexually-transmitted diseases such as AIDS.

The rapid worldwide rate of increase in AIDS continues (currently 26 percent a year) and, in its latest report, the World Health Organization showed that over one and a quarter million adult cases had been reported from 193 countries as a result of the pandemic.[45] Allowing for under-diagnosis, incomplete reporting, and reporting delay, the true figure is estimated to be about six million, and approximately 17 million people are estimated to have the human immunodeficiency virus (HIV) which causes the disease.

The World Health Organization extrapolates for each country the per capita prevalence of HIV. The results for 1996 are truly stunning. Forty-seven countries are currently estimated to have one percent or more of their sexually active population living with HIV. Thirty-seven of these countries are in sub-Saharan Africa and seven are in the Caribbean. A sampling: Botswana, Zimbabwe, Zambia and Uganda have upwards of 20 percent or more of their sexually active population living with HIV; South Africa, Kenya, Mozambique and Zaire have from three to ten percent living with HIV; in the Caribbean, Haiti, Bahamas, Barbados, and Belize have two percent or more of their population infected; and Jamaica, Bermuda, and the Dominican Republic have more than one percent.

U.S. data show that African-Americans have rates similar to their counterparts in black Africa and the black Caribbean, with three percent of black men and one percent of black women living with HIV.[46] This survey, appearing in *Science*, drew correspondence to the effect that "race" was not causal to the incidence rates but was merely a marker for social factors such as poverty, which were the real causes. The author of the report replied, however, noting that (1) even with socioeconomic indicators controlled, sexually transmitted infections remained higher among African-Americans than among other groups, and (2) "cultural variations in behavior," distinct from socioeconomic status, were part of the complex web of causation.[47] None of the correspondents pointed to the racial distribution elsewhere in the world nor to the fact that in Africa, it is high socioeconomic status that puts people at risk, mainly by increasing their access to sexual partners. Throughout the world, the virus must be considered endemic to black populations.

Heritability of Racial Differences

The worldwide consistency of the Oriental-white-black gradient on so many variables makes it very likely that some of the differences are genetic. Of course, environmental factors such as poor nutrition, and the presence of parasites like tapeworms do have effects on brain size and behavior. No one is arguing that the racial differences are 100 percent genetic. Instead, the argument is between "hereditarians" like Arthur Jensen, Michael Levin, Richard Lynn, and me who hold to a mixed genetic-environmental model, say about 50 percent genetic and 50 percent environmental, and the "egalitarians" who hold, in effect, that racial differences are 100 percent environmental.

Theories of racial differences based on 100 percent cultural transmission have formidable problems accounting for the physiological traits such as speed of dental and physical maturation, brain size, gamete production, and testosterone production as well as the consistency of the racial rankings across time and culture. Direct evidence for between-group heritabilities also exists. For example, the racial differences in multiple birthing are independently heritable through the race of the mother and not through the race of the father, as found in Oriental/white crosses in Hawaii and white/black crosses in Brazil.[44]

Estimates of the heritability of IQ among whites routinely range from 40 percent to 80 percent. Similar heritabilities are also found among black Americans, Oriental Americans, Koreans, and the Japanese in Japan. In a study of the heritability of cranial size among 236 pairs of adolescent twins, both blacks and whites, Travis Osborne and I found the genetic contribution ranged from 38 percent to 51 percent depending on particular adjustments for body size.[48] It seems reasonable to generalize these high within-group heritabilities to the between-group differences.

More direct evidence for the heritability of racial differences comes from adoption studies. Korean and Vietnamese children adopted into white American and white Belgian homes grow to have IQs ten or more points higher than their adoptive national norms.[49-51] As babies, many of these children had been hospitalized for malnutrition. By contrast, black and mixed-race (black/white) children adopted into white middle-class families typically perform at a lower level than white siblings with whom they have been raised. One well-known study is the Minnesota Transracial Adoption Study (see Table 2, next page). By age 17, adopted white children had an average IQ of 106, an aptitude based on national norms at the 59th percentile, and a class rank at the 54th percentile; adopted mixed-race children had an average IQ of 99, an aptitude at the 53rd percentile, and a class rank at the 40th percentile; and adopted black children had an average IQ of 89, an aptitude at the 42nd percentile, and a class rank at the 36th percentile.[52]

Comparison of Black, Mixed-Race, and White Adopted and Biological Children Raised In White Middle-Class Families

Children's Background	Age 7 IQ	Age 17 IQ
Adopted, 2 black biological parents	97	89
Adopted, 1 white, 1 black biological parent	109	99
Adopted, 2 white biological parents	112	106
Nonadopted, 2 white biological parents	117	109

Children's Background	Age 17 School Achievement GPA	Class Rank	Age 17 School Aptitude Based on National Norms
Adopted, 2 black parents	2.1	36	42
Adopted, 1 black parent	2.2	40	53
Adopted, 2 white parents	2.8	54	59
Nonadopted, 2 white parents	3.0	64	69

Based on data from Weinberg, Scarr and Waldman (ref. 52).

As shown in the above table, the mixed-race children had scores intermediate to the "all-white" and "all-black" children. Numerous studies have shown similar results with lighter skin typically correlating with higher IQ. William Shockley estimated that for low-IQ black populations, there is a one-point increase in average "genetic" IQ for each one percent of Caucasian ancestry, with diminishing returns as an IQ of 100 is reached.[53] Overall, using blood tests and DNA markers, studies show that African-Americans have about 25 percent European genes.[54] It is interesting to note in this regard that Cape Coloreds, a mixed-race population in South Africa, average an IQ of 85, mid-way between non-mixed black South Africans with an IQ of 70 and white South Africans with an IQ of 100.

More technical evidence for the genetic basis of the racial differences in IQ comes from studies using differential heritabilities. Some items and subtests are more genetically influenced than are others. The more genetically influenced the subtest, the more it differentiates between blacks and whites. A very similar relation is found with the general factor of intelligence (known as g) showing that different IQ tests tend to be related. More g-loaded tests also tend to be more heritable. Although heritability and g-loadedness are conceptually distinct, both differentiate blacks from whites. Thus, while the white/black IQ gap averages 15 points, the difference is substantially more pronounced on tests of high heritability and high g than it is on tests of low heritability and low g.[55-57] Here is a situation in which environmental and genetic hypotheses predict opposite outcomes. Environmental theory predicts racial differences will be greater on more culturally influenced tests whereas genetic theory predicts racial differences will be greater on more heritable and g-loaded tests.

Evolutionary Origins of Race Differences

Evolutionary selection pressures are different in the hot African savanna where Negroids evolved than they are in the cold Arctic, where Mongoloids evolved. The modern "African Eve" theory of human origins posits a beginning in Africa some 200,000 years ago, an exodus through the Middle East with an African/non-African split about 110,000 years ago, and a Caucasoid/Mongoloid split about 41,000 years ago.[58] This evolutionary sequence fits with and helps to explain how and why the variables cluster. The further north the populations migrated out of Africa, the more they encountered the cognitively demanding problems of gathering and storing food, acquiring shelter, making clothes, and raising children successfully during prolonged winters. As the original African populations evolved into present-day Caucasoids and Mongoloids, they did so in the direction of larger brains, slower rates of maturation, and lower levels of sex hormone with concomitant reductions in sexual potency, aggressiveness and impulsiveness, and increases in family stability, advance planning, self-control, rule following, and longevity.

To my mind, little or no reasonable doubt remains about the genetic basis for at least some of the racial differences. I am aware of no environmental factor able to explain either the consistency of the international racial pattern across so many diverse variables or the tradeoff between brain size and gamete production in which people of East Asian ancestry average the largest brains and the lowest twinning rate, people of African ancestry average the smallest brains and the highest twinning rate, and people of European ancestry average intermediately in both. Only gene-based life-history theories predicting tradeoffs between parental care and reproductive effort fit all of the data.

Conclusion

Recognizing that the pattern in achievement, crime, and family organization is not unique to the United States but occurs internationally shows the need for a more general (genetic-evolutionary) theory than the particularized explanations typically provided. The behavioral profile of blacks in America is like those for blacks in Africa and the Caribbean and so cannot be due to "white racism" or other cultural features unique to the U.S. Similarly, whites and Asians in America behave like their counterparts elsewhere in the world. Traditional environmental explanations based on Asian family strength and African poverty are themselves explained by an evolutionary perspective.

Policy analysts need to rethink attitudes about race differences and acknowledge their international distribution and genetic basis. Based on the evidence, two important predictions can be made about the future course of world history. First, with respect to economic and scientific achievements, the Oriental populations of the Pacific Rim must be expected to continue to grow in accomplishments until they eventually equal or outdistance the predominantly Caucasian populations of North America and Western Europe. Second, with respect to the HIV and AIDS pandemic, mortality among black Americans must soon be expected in large proportions. Given the costs involved in providing custodial care, it may be the AIDS catastrophe that finally breaks down the taboo on discussing the genetic basis of race.

References

1. Myrdal, G. (1944/1996). *An American Dilemma: The Negro Problem and Modern Democracy*. (Vols I & II). New Brunswick, NJ: Transaction. (First published in 1944 by Harper & Row).

2. Rushton, J. P. (1995). *Race, Evolution, and Behavior: A Life-History Perspective*. New Brunswick, NJ: Transaction.

3. Snyderman, M., & Rothman, S. (1987). Survey of expert opinion on intelligence and aptitude testing. *American Psychologist, 42*, 137-144.

4. Snyderman, M., & Rothman, S. (1988). *The IQ Controversy*, The Media, and Public Policy. New Brunswick, NJ: Transaction Publishers.

5. Herrnstein, R. J., & Murray, C. (1994). *The Bell Curve*. New York: Free Press.

6. Fraser, S. (1995). *The Bell Curve Wars*. New York: Basic Books.

7. Jacoby, R., & Glauberman, N. (1995). *The Bell Curve Debate*. New York: Random House.

8. Jensen, A. R. (1973). *Educability and Group Differences*. London: Methuen.

9. Jensen, A. R. (1980). *Bias in Mental Testing*. New York: Free Press.

10. Lynn, R. (1982). IQ in Japan and the United States shows a growing disparity. *Nature, 297,* 222-223.

11. Lynn, R. (1991). Race differences in intelligence: A global perspective. *Mankind Quarterly, 31,* 255-296.

12. Blinkhorn, S. (1994). Willow, titwillow, titwillow! [Review of the books *The Bell Curve, Measuring the Mind, and Race, Evolution, and Behavior*]. *Nature, 372,* 417-419.

13. Kamin, L. (1995). Lies, damned lies, and statistics. In R. Jacoby and N. Glauberman (Eds.), *The Bell Curve Debate* (pp. 81-105). New York: Random House.

14. Owen, K. (1992). The suitability of Raven's Standard Progressive Matrices for various groups in South Africa. *Personality and Individual Differences, 13,* 149-159.

15. Zindi, F. (1994). Differences in performance. *The Psychologist, 7,* 549-552.

16. Lynn, R. (1994). The intelligence of Ethiopian immigrant and Israeli adolescents. *International Journal of Psychology, 29,* 55-56.

17. Neisser, U., Boodoo, G., Bouchard, T. J. Jr., Boykin, A. W., Brody, N., Ceci, S. J., Halpern, D. F., Loehlin, J. C., Perloff, R., Sternberg, R. J., & Urbina, S. (1996). Intelligence: Knowns and unknowns. *American Psychologist, 51,* 77-101.

18. Lynn, R., & Shigehisa, T. (1991). Reaction times and intelligence: A comparison of Japanese and British children. *Journal of Biosocial Science, 23,* 409-416.

19. Jensen, A. R. (1993). Spearman's hypothesis tested with chronometric information processing tasks. *Intelligence, 17*, 47-77.

20. Jensen, A. R., & Whang, P. A. (1993). Reaction times and intelligence. *Journal of Biosocial Science, 25*, 397-410.

21. Rushton, J. P., & Ankney, C. D. (1996). Brain size and cognitive ability: Correlations with age, sex, social class and race. *Psychonomic Bulletin and Review, 3*, 21-36.

22. Ho, K. C., Roessmann, U., Straumfjord, J. V., & Monroe, G. (1980). Analysis of brain weight. I and II. *Archives of Pathology and Laboratory Medicine, 104*, 635-645.

23. Beals, K. L., Smith, C. L. & Dodd, S. M. (1984). Brain size, cranial morphology, climate, and time machines. *Current Anthropology, 25*, 301-330.

24. Rushton, J. P. (1992). Cranial capacity related to sex, rank, and race in a stratified random sample of 6,325 U.S. military personnel. *Intelligence, 16*, 401-413.

25. Rushton, J. P. (1994). Sex and race differences in cranial capacity from International Labour Office data. *Intelligence, 19*, 281-294.

26. Harvey, I., Persaud, R., Ron, M. A., Baker, G., & Murray, R. M. (1994). Volumetric MRI measurements in bipolars compared with schizophrenics and healthy controls. *Psychological Medicine, 24*, 689-699.

27. Broman, S. H., Nichols, P. L., Shaughnessy, P. & Kennedy, W. (1987). *Retardation in Young Children*. Hillsdale, NJ: Erlbaum.

28. Whitney, G. (1995). Ideology and censorship in behavior genetics. *Mankind Quarterly, 35*, 327-342.

29. Wilson, J. Q., & Herrnstein, R. J. (1985). *Crime and Human Nature*. New York: Simon & Schuster.

30. Ontario. (1996). *Report of the Commission on Systemic Racism in the Ontario Criminal Justice System*. Ministry of the Solicitor-General and Correctional Services. Toronto, Ontario: Queen's Printer for Ontario.

31. Rushton, J. P. (1990). Race and crime: A reply to Roberts and Gabor. *Canadian Journal of Criminology, 32*, 315-334.

32. Rushton, J. P. (1995). Race and crime: International data for 1989-90. *Psychological Reports, 76*, 307-312.

33. Draper, P. (1989). African marriage systems: Perspectives from evolutionary ecology. *Ethology and Sociobiology, 10*, 145-169.

34. Booth, A., & Osgood, D. W. (1993). The influence of testosterone on deviance in adulthood: Assessing and extending the relationship. *Criminology, 31*, 93-117.

35. Ellis, L., & Nyborg, H. (1992). Racial/ethnic variations in male testosterone levels: A probable contributor to group differences in health. *Steroids, 57,* 72-75.

36. Polednak, A. P. (1989). *Racial and Ethnic Differences in Disease.* Oxford: Oxford University Press.

37. Tremblay, R. E., & Baillargeon, L. (1984). Les difficultés de comportement d'enfants immigrants dans les classes d'accueil, au préscolaire. *Canadian Journal of Education, 9,* 154-170.

38. Rushton, J. P. (1985). Differential K theory and race differences in E and N. *Personality and Individual Differences, 6,* 769-770.

39. Niswander, K. R., & Gordon, M. (1972). *The Women and Their Pregnancies.* Philadelphia, PA: Saunders.

40. Papiernik, E., Cohen, H., Richard, A., de Oca, M. M., & Feingold, J. (1986). Ethnic differences in duration of pregnancy. *Annals of Human Biology, 13,* 259-265.

41. Bayley, N. (1965). Comparisons of mental and motor test scores for ages 1-15 months by sex, birth order, race, geographic location, and education of parents. *Child Development, 36,* 379-411.

42. Freedman, D. G. (1974). *Human Infancy.* New York: Halsted.

43. Freedman, D. G. (1979). *Human Sociobiology.* New York: Free Press.

44. Bulmer, M. G. (1970). *The Biology of Twinning in Man.* Oxford: Clarendon Press.

45. World Health Organization. (1996). Global Programme on AIDS. *The Current Global Situation of the HIV/AIDS Pandemic.* Geneva, Switzerland: World Health Organization.

46. Rosenberg, P. S. (1995). Scope of the AIDS epidemic in the United States. *Science, 270,* 1372-1375.

47. Rosenberg, P. S. (1996). AIDS and ethnicity. *Science, 271,* 1480-1481.

48. Rushton, J. P., & Osborne, R. T. (1995). Genetic and environmental contributions to cranial capacity estimated in black and white adolescents. *Intelligence, 20,* 1-13.

49. Clark, E. A., & Hanisee, J. (1982). Intellectual and adaptive performance of Asian children in adoptive American settings. *Developmental Psychology, 18,* 595-599.

50. Frydman, M., & Lynn, R. (1989). The intelligence of Korean children adopted in Belgium. *Personality and Individual Differences, 10,* 1323-1326.

51. Winick, M., Meyer, K. K., & Harris, R. C. (1975). Malnutrition and environmental enrichment by early adoption. *Science, 190,* 1173-1175.

52. Weinberg, R. A., Scarr, S., & Waldman, I. D. (1992). The Minnesota Transracial Adoption Study: A follow-up of IQ test performance at adolescence. *Intelligence, 16*, 117-135.
53. Shockley, W. (1973). Variance of Caucasian admixture in Negro populations, pigmentation variablity, and IQ. *Proceedings of the National Academy of Sciences, U.S.A., 70*, 2180a.
54. Chakraborty, R., Kamboh, M. I., Nwankwo, M., & Ferrell, R. E. (1992). Caucasion genes in American blacks: New data. *American Journal of Human Genetics, 50*, 145-155.
55. Jensen, A. R. (1985). The nature of the black-white difference on various psychometic tests: Spearman's hypothesis. *Behavioral and Brain Sciences, 8*, 193-263.
56. Jensen, A. R. (1987). Further evidence for Spearman's hypothesis concerning the black-white differences on psychometric tests. *Behavioral and Brain Sciences, 10*, 512-519.
57. Rushton, J. P. (1989). Japanese inbreeding depression scores: Predictors of cognitive differences between blacks and whites. *Intelligence, 13*, 43-51.
58. Stringer, C. B., & Andrews, P. (1988). Genetic and fossil evidence for the origin of modern humans. *Science, 239*, 1263-1268.

Author's Note. This paper is based on presentations to the Conference on *The Bell Curve–Retrospect and Prospect* (Washington, DC, April 14-16, 1996), to the American Renaissance Conference (Louisville, KY, May 26, 1996), and to the European Sociobiological Society at Alfred University (Alfred, NY, July 24, 1996). It draws on my book *Race, Evolution, and Behavior* (1995).

☾☽

CRSO

Equality Unmasked

Samuel Francis

A good deal of water has gone under the bridge since the first
American Renaissance conference met in Atlanta in 1994. At
that time, neither *The Bell Curve* nor Professor Rushton's
book, *Race, Evolution and Behavior* had been published, nor even the
rather less immortal contributions of the learned D'Souza. I felt then, in
the aftermath of the Atlanta conference and when these books were
published the following fall, rather optimistic about the progress being
made by those who sought a re-evaluation of the role of race, but I have
to say that today my optimism is considerably more muted. The bitterly
hostile reaction to *The Bell Curve* and Professor Rushton's work, the
dishonest and cowardly treatment of the *American Renaissance* conference in D'Souza's book, the crusade mounted in the press against this
conference, similar crusades against talk show host Bob Grant in New
York and against British psychologist Christopher Brand's new book,
The g Factor, in Great Britain, and the difficulty that both Professor
Michael Levin and apparently Arthur Jensen have experienced in finding publishers for their own major new books–all lead me to believe
that we, or certainly I, had seriously underestimated the resistance that
frank and serious discussion of race would encounter.

I have little more to tell you about race, and certainly less than what
Professors Rushton and Levin and the other speakers can tell you, so
what I am going to talk about today is this very resistance that we encounter, why it exists and why it seems to be so powerful, and perhaps
how we can meet and overcome it. I am going to start off with an account of the systematic harassment of two of our speakers today,
Rushton and Levin, and I choose them for several reasons–partly because they are present and can comment or criticize my account as they
see fit, partly because their stories offer instructive lessons for the conclusions that I am going to draw, and partly because both of them have
displayed a great amount of courage and commitment to their beliefs
and scientific findings, and I think it is advisable that this audience ap-
preciate what some of us have to go through in order to provide you
with the edification and entertainment of this weekend.

My account of their experiences is drawn largely from Roger Pearson's book, *Race, Intelligence and Bias in Academe*, which is a study of how various academics and scientists who have violated taboos about race have been systematically harassed by the political left over the last 20 years or so. But I am going to end up with an account of the ongoing vilification of this conference in the press, especially the local newspaper the *Louisville Courier-Journal*, and show how that campaign has been organized. Finally, I will try to draw some conclusions about why these crusades are effective and how they can be resisted and overcome.

In the Rushton case, Professor Rushton's problems began soon after he delivered a paper at the January, 1989 convention of the American Association for the Advancement of Science (AAAS) in San Francisco. His paper was a précis of the research on racial differences that he later published and will discuss this evening, and it immediately generated attacks in the media. The *Toronto Star* reported in a headline soon after his speech that "Canadian Professor's Study Stirs Uproar at Conference," while two days later it carried a story headlined "Theory 'Racist': Prof has Scholars Boiling." This kind of news coverage and worse continued for some months and was characterized by reporters seeking to elicit statements of condemnation of Rushton or his research from his colleagues or from officials of the AAAS, and by soliciting reactions from various leftist groups in Canada and on the Western Ontario campus. Rushton's own efforts to debate or explain his theory further on television were probably not helpful, since the debate format was usually stacked against him and dwelt on the supposed political rather than the actual scientific meaning of his theory, and on one occasion he was greeted with a hostile and jeering audience of some 2,000.

By early February, the Mayor of London, Ontario had formed a committee to "investigate" Rushton and his theories to determine whether they violated Canadian law. As many of you perhaps know, Canadian democracy enjoys a law known as the Race Relations Act that criminalizes anyone who "willfully promotes hatred against any identifiable group" and subjects such criminals to a maximum sentence of two years in prison. At first, apparently, the major demand was that Rushton simply be dismissed from his teaching position, and only later in March did the Attorney General of Ontario, dedicated to bringing dangerous criminals to justice, order a police investigation.

The police forces of Ontario and Toronto formed a joint special force on "Pornography and Hate Literature" that was supposed to interview Rushton and some of his academic supervisors at the university for the purpose of discovering whether he had violated the law. The investigation took six months and eventually concluded that while he had not violated the law, "it is the overwhelming opinion of academics questioned that in many cases your conclusions . . . have been drawn on misinterpreted and/or questionable data. This has resulted in your presentation to the AAAS falling noticeably short of expected professional standards." Apparently, in Canada, it is the business of the police to reach conclusions on matters of scientific interest. The audience, which by now perhaps suspects that there is a dangerous criminal in our midst, will no doubt be relieved to learn that the Attorney General of Ontario then held a press conference at which he graciously announced that Rushton was "loony but not criminal."

Yet at the same time the press campaign and the police investigation were going on, university authorities on Rushton's own campus also chimed in with denunciations of his ideas. The dean of social science at the university published a letter in the university newspaper in which she attacked Rushton's theory, and in July, 1989, he was given an "unsatisfactory" rating on his three-year performance evaluation by his department chairman, and denied a usually routine pay increase. Under university rules, teachers who receive such evaluations three times in a row can be dismissed from their jobs. Now the fact is that Professor Rushton holds a doctorate in social psychology, was the author of five books and more than a 100 articles in scholarly journals, and held a Guggenheim Fellowship. Rushton appealed the evaluation to the dean's office and asked that she recuse herself because she had already published her views of Rushton. She refused to recuse herself and her office upheld the department chairman's evaluation. Rushton then appealed the evaluation through a university grievance procedure, and, arguing on the basis of his credentials and also that during the three years for which he was evaluated he had published 30 articles and two books and received the Guggenheim, he won a reversal of the negative evaluation.

When Rushton returned to teaching in 1990, local agitators threatened to disrupt his classes to prevent him from teaching, and the dean ordered that he not be permitted to teach his classes in person. He was supposed to make videotapes of his lectures, and students were supposed to listen to them in a private room in which he could not be present. Questions were to be called in by phone. Rushton again appealed this ruling and won, but the dean appealed the decision. Eventually, the department decided to ignore the dean's ruling and return Rushton to teaching his classes in person.

In 1991, Rushton's classes were disrupted on at least three occasions by protesters and he was physically attacked on one such occasion. Despite warnings from the university that it would prosecute disrupters, it had not done so by the spring of 1991, and student protesters, mainly made up of African or Caribbean students or New Left elements, continued to disrupt his classes and on one occasion in March, 1991, actually disrupted the Provincial Parliament. I am sure Professor Rushton has enjoyed similar adventures in recent years, but my information about them ends in 1991.

Prof. Levin's experiences at the City College of New York resemble those of Professor Rushton. Levin's original crime against humanity consisted of publishing a letter in the *New York Times* in 1988 arguing that shopkeepers had the right not to open their doors to black males if they feared robbery. The publication of such shocking opinions apparently mobilized cadres of student leftists to break down the door of the university president, who admitted that the students had the right to picket Levin's classes. Professor Levin was considerately provided with a bodyguard.

The group known as the International Committee against Racism (InCAR), a Maoist group, circulated Levin's letter to the *Times* on campus, but the controversy was further excited by an article Levin published in an Australian magazine called *Quadrant* in which he apparently argued that the decline of American education was in part due to the rise of radical feminism and to affirmative action and its promotion of lower-IQ black students. The reaction against this article came mainly from the faculty rather than from student activists, and on October 20, 1988 the faculty senate voted to condemn Levin's article as "racist" and as "lacking cogency or empirical support." Levin was given only three hours notice that censure was to be considered and was not able to be present at the debate. Soon afterward, the university president, who presumably by this time had gotten his door fixed, issued a letter commending the faculty for their intrepid denunciation of racism and beamed that he had been "a proud witness to the discussion and debate" and that the resolution reflected the university's commitment to "equality."

This was followed by Levin's being told by the Dean of Humanities and the philosophy department chairman that Levin should voluntarily withdraw from teaching his introductory philosophy course, and if he didn't voluntarily withdraw, the chairman would come to the first class and invite the students to transfer to another section. Believing this would be temporary, Levin agreed to this proposal, but later learned that it was meant to be permanent and would be extended to any required course that Levin taught. This kind of restriction severely limits a teacher's ability to recruit students for advanced work and represented a long-term threat to Levin's academic career.

Meanwhile, plans for the inquisition proceeded briskly, with the president of the university writing a letter urging the faculty senate to form a committee to investigate faculty members for "bias-related activities." The senate refused to do so on the lucid grounds that such a committee would have a "chilling effect" on academic freedom, if not on their own careers, but the president continued to badger for such a committee and in several interviews expressed frustration that he was unable to break Levin's tenure and fire him altogether.

Levin, meanwhile, continued to commit yet more crimes against humanity. When the American Philosophical Association concluded that blacks were underrepresented in teaching philosophy, Levin published a letter in the Proceedings of the APA arguing that the reason had to do with the lower black IQ. This led the humanities dean at his school to send a letter to each of Levin's students warning them that their professor harbored what the dean called "controversial" views about race and sex and offering them an alternative section if they were unable to cope with the trauma of being exposed to controversy in the course of studying philosophy. Finally, the president got down to business by forming a committee to inquire into whether Levin had engaged in "conduct unbecoming a faculty member," a phrase usually associated with efforts to break tenure and dismiss the faculty member. Three of the seven members of the committee had earlier signed a petition stating that Levin was unfit to teach. In March, 1990, a mob invaded Levin's classroom, earning the praise of the president for its "restraint." In the event, the inquisition against Levin did not succeed, in part because he eventually took successful legal action against the president and the humanities dean, as had Rushton against the Toronto *Star*. But as Pearson comments in his conclusion about the Levin case:

> In many ways the most revealing and disappointing aspect of the Levin affair was the complete failure of his colleagues, or the media which covered it, to discuss the validity of Levin's views. At no point did any newspaper publish the relevant IQ data, or invite competent psychometrists to comment on it. The head of the psychology department refused Levin's invitation to debate his claims. By attacking his academic freedom and defining battle lines along

academic-freedom lines, academic egalitarians once again managed
to obscure the real core of the issue.[1]

Now, there is a common pattern in both of these cases, and I think
in several others, that needs to be called attention to. What happens
when an academic violates a taboo on race is that first the media broadcast and typically misrepresent it and then the professional left, usually
on campus–either racial minorities who feel aggrieved or white Marxists–moves into battle by invading classrooms, staging protests. prayer
vigils, disruptions, demonstrations, and all the rest of it. But for the
most part, even though that phase of the attack is the most visible and
the most publicized, it is not the heart of the academic criminal's problems. The heart of his problem comes from lack of sufficient support
from his colleagues and supervisors or from their active hostility. De-
rogatory and dismissive comments on the academic's ideas can serve to
harm his career and professional stature. Disciplinary action by chair-
men, deans, committees, and university presidents can actually cost
him his job or at least disrupt and subvert his academic work in teaching and research. It makes sense for Marxists and even minority students to be offended by ideas they regard as "racist" and even, up to a
point, to protest such ideas, and, again up to a point, that is their right.
What makes far less sense is for professional academics and academic
administrators to involve themselves in the controversy against the academic taboo-breaker and to devote so much of their energies to punish-
ing or silencing him.

And what this pattern, as well as the general hysteria that informs
the reaction to any violation of taboos concerning racial equality, point
to, in my view, is that what we are dealing with in egalitarianism today
is not a rational belief; what we are dealing with in egalitarianism is an
ideology that serves various social and political and even psychological
functions. In fact, egalitarianism since the Progressive Era of the early
20th century and especially since the New Deal has become an unofficial and increasingly an official ideology of the system in which we
live, of the government, the dominant culture, and even the economy of
the United States and the Western world. Egalitarianism has become an
ideology that protects, serves, and rationalizes the interests of the elites
that hold power in Western society, just as doctrines like the Divine
Right of Kings served the interests of monarchies and aristocracies before the French Revolution.

Pearson points to this role of egalitarianism in his chapter on the
Rushton case when he writes:

Rushton's research had carried him into an area of direct economic and political significance: his findings had uncovered flaws in the established version of environmentalist social science testimony on which massive government programs had been built in both Canada and the U.S.A. These not only provided for a massive redistribution of wealth and reverse discrimination in employment, but had provided a vested interest for millions of beneficiaries. His findings also threatened the well-being of organizations that had been built on the surplus funds which could be culled from supervising this redistribution of wealth, and also had potentially adverse implications for the immigration "industry." Little did Rushton realize that his seemingly innocent research would stir up such a tempest. Those on the Left knew the crucial importance of the data he was studying, and of the need to keep the public from accepting his opinions–as well as preventing other scholars from daring to speak their minds on the issues involved. [2]

I think that understanding egalitarianism as the ideology of elites is important for several reasons. In the first place, it puts the Marxists and radicals of the left in an entirely different light from the one in which they like to present themselves, that of rebels against the system. Invariably, when Marxist groups protest against "racism" they argue that "racism is the tool of capitalism," that a capitalist ruling class promotes racism in order to justify the exploitation of non-whites and to keep the white and non-white proletariats divided. But in reality there is no truth whatsoever in this theory. If it were true, we would expect academics like Rushton and Levin, Arthur Jensen and Richard Herrnstein, to have received millions in grants from large corporations and foundations. In fact they receive little or nothing, and the grants those institutions do make do not support hereditarian views of social problems but rather environmentalist and egalitarian views. It was, after all the Carnegie Foundation that provided Gunnar Myrdal with $300,000 to produce *An American Dilemma*, for years the bible of racial egalitarian environmentalism.

The truth is that when Marxists and self-described radicals denounce what they call "racism" they are in fact acting as the ideological vanguard of the real elites who hold power and possess enormous vested interests in egalitarianism and environmentalism. It is the radical egalitarians and anti-hereditarians who are the real running dogs of the system, not those who challenge egalitarianism and environmentalism, and it is the hereditarians like Rushton and Levin who are the real radicals or even revolutionaries who challenge the lies and mythologies in which entrenched powers always mask themselves.

In the second place, understanding egalitarianism as the ideology of the system and the elites that run it ought to alter our view of how the system and its elites actually operate. Most elites in history have always had a vested interest in preserving the societies they rule, and that is why most elites have been conservative–the British aristocracy up to the 20th century is a fairly typical example of such a conservative elite. But the elite that has come to power in the United States and the Western world in this century actually has a vested interest in managing and manipulating social change, in transforming the society it rules. Political analyst Kevin Phillips pointed this out in his 1975 book, *Mediacracy*, which is a study of the emergence of what he calls the "new knowledge elite," the members of which:

> approach society from a new vantage point. . . . Change does not threaten the affluent intelligentsia of the Post-Industrial Society the way it threatened the landowners and industrialists of the New Deal. On the contrary, change is as essential to the knowledge sector as inventory turnover is to a merchant or a manufacturer. Change keeps up demand for the product (research, news, theory, and technology). Post-Industrialism, a knowledge elite, and accelerated social change appear to go hand in hand. . . . The new knowledge elite does not preserve and protect existing traditions and institutions. On the contrary, far more than previous new classes, the knowledge elite has sought to modify or replace traditional institutions with new relationships and power centers.[3]

And egalitarianism and environmentalism serve this need to create and manage social change perfectly. Traditional institutions can be depicted not only as "unequal" and "oppressive" but also as "pathological," requiring the social and economic therapy that only the "knowledge elite" is skilled enough to design and apply. The interests of the knowledge elite in managing social change happen to be entirely consistent not only with the agendas of the hard left but also with the grievances and demands of various racial and ethnic groups that view "racism" and "prejudice" as obstacles to their own advancement, so that what we see is an alliance between the new elites and organized racial and ethnic minorities to undermine and displace the traditional institutions and beliefs of white Euro-American society, which just happen to be the power centers of older elites based on wealth, land, and status. This process of displacement or dispossession is always described as "progressive," "liberating," or "diversifying," when in fact it merely helps consolidate the dominance of a new class and weaken the power and interests of its rivals.

Furthermore, what this understanding of the real meaning of egalitarianism leads to is that when we see university deans and presidents "caving in" to the demands of the hard left, they are not really displaying traits of weakness and appeasement. Universities are the breeding grounds of egalitarianism and its applications to society by the elites, and hence they occupy a special and strategic place in the functioning of the system. If the ideology of egalitarianism were abandoned, many of the functions that universities now perform in the way of research and much of what their faculties do in designing egalitarian social programs and therapy would become obsolete. When the universities "cave in" to the left, therefore, they are simply pursuing their own interests, which are to preserve the political ideology of egalitarianism intact and suppress or silence those who dissent from it, and they are in fact behaving like any elite, like the French aristocracy of the 18th century, for example, when it punished Enlightenment writers who challenged aristocratic ideologies.

Their behavior appears to be weak or degenerate or renegade to us because we look at their conduct from the point of view of those who believe the consequences of egalitarianism are harmful and have to live with those consequences and also because most of us continue to harbor the illusion that the elites that now prevail in this country and much of the Western world are still in some sense "our" elites, that they represent us, when in fact they mainly represent themselves and their class interests and the ideology and agendas that serve those interests.

I think understanding egalitarianism today as the ideology of a dominant elite that uses it to serve its own interests may suggest ways in which we could more successfully confront the ideology and those it serves. In the past, most of those who have challenged egalitarianism in one form or another have done so through what we might call rationalistic means–that is, they have tried to cite scientific or empirical evidence logically assembled to support the challenge. Certainly that is an important and indeed crucial element of the challenge, but whatever its rational and scientific merits, it has not been enough. As Pearson points out, none of Levin's critics and not many of Rushton's either were interested in debating their ideas or dealing with their scientific validity. Of course not; what their critics were interested in was power and in preventing Rushton, Levin, and others from challenging their power. And that is exactly the point at which they should be attacked and exposed.

What we need to do, in addition to building the scientific and scholarly case against egalitarianism and environmentalism, is to take a page from the book of the left itself, to expose those who resist scientific evidence and who respond to it only with lies and repression as the beneficiaries of the egalitarian ideology they are trying to protect. We need to show that an entire political and economic industry gains wealth and power from egalitarian environmental ideology and, in a word, "unmask" or "deconstruct" those interests, and we need in particular to show how Americans–as taxpayers, as crime victims, as job and college applicants, and frankly simply as whites–are being exploited and victimized by the lie of equality and the power structure that rests on it. We need to show also how the media conglomerates, which with universities are sort of the belly of the beast of the new knowledge elite, systematically depict whites and their traditional cultural symbols in inferior, demeaning, and villainous roles and how they deliberately distort news about race and scientific racial research against whites.

One example of this comes from the crusade against Bob Grant in New York, which was largely conducted by a group that calls itself "FAIR," for "Fairness and Accuracy in Reporting." FAIR poses as a "watchdog" of the press, but the quickest glance at the materials it produces shows that it is in fact a hard-left political battery dedicated to ridding the media of anyone to the right of Tom Brokaw. It has produced "dossiers" on Rush Limbaugh to prove he is not a reliable source of information and has produced a similar document on Pat Buchanan to "document" his "racism" and "extremism," but I am unable to identify any such "dossier" produced by FAIR on any liberal or left-wing commentator. One of its abiding bugaboos is the corporate "concentration of media ownership," and it loves to thump its chest about its passion to "invigorate the First Amendment by advocating for [sic] greater plurality and diversity in the media" and defending "working journalists when they are muzzled." As a working journalist who was muzzled, I might have made use of FAIR's talents, but for some reason I have heard nothing from them.

But Mr. Grant did hear from them. On March 31 of this year, FAIR ran a quarter-page ad on the op-ed page of the Sunday *New York Times* in the form of an open letter to Michael Eisner of the Walt Disney Company, which was the new corporate parent of Mr. Grant's station. The ad claimed that Mr. Grant on his program had promoted "the white supremacist *American Renaissance* conference in Louisville" and demanded of Mr. Eisner, "Is it the policy of the Walt Disney Company to allow hosts on its stations to make racial slurs?" and "Is it Disney's policy to allow the promotion of white supremacist groups on its stations?" Though FAIR did not explicitly demand Grant's firing, it was clear that was the goal it had in mind. So much for "invigorating the First Amendment."

I will comment only briefly on the falsity of the description of *American Renaissance* and this conference, let alone me, as "white supremacist," a term none of us has ever applied to ourselves and one which we have explicitly, publicly, and repeatedly rejected. FAIR did not bother to cite any of several published letters by me to major newspapers rejecting this term.

Now not only is FAIR neither fair nor accurate in what it jokingly calls its "reporting," but also it managed to reach all the way out into the boondocks of Louisville to induce reporter David Heath of the *Louisville Courier* to swallow its bait and then regurgitate it in the form of "news articles" here, articles that are transparently inaccurate and equally transparently based on FAIR's propaganda. It turns out that while FAIR whines and grouses about corporate "concentration of media ownership," an issue with which I am substantially in agreement, FAIR actually receives a good deal of its own cash from such concentrations of mega-money as the MacArthur Foundation and the Turner Foundation in Atlanta, the tax-exempt preserve of multimillionaire media czar Ted Turner and his wife, the famous North Vietnamese patriot herself, as well as from Barbra Streisand's foundation. And while poor little old FAIR is whining about "concentration of media ownership," it's interesting to note that it was in the *Louisville Courier-Journal,* owned by the humongous Gannett chain, that it was able to get its unfair and inaccurate misreporting into print and also that Bob Grant's job was largely safe as long as his station was owned by the relatively small ABC/Capital Cities company but went down the drain pipes not long after Eisner-World took it over. FAIR is in fact dependent on large sums of cash from tax-exempt foundations run by wealthy leftists and assorted airheads, and its claims to resist media concentration, to champion "muzzled reporters," and to "invigorate" the First Amendment and freedom of expression are all simply lies that mask its real role as a tool of the real elites that have come to power in this country.

Finally, in addition to unmasking the real role of egalitarianism as a device of power, we need to take yet another page from the book of the left in mustering the courage to stand up and speak up for what we believe in, to develop the kind of solidarity against which lies and repression cannot stand. We do not yet have that kind of solidarity, and the result is that we are picked off one by one whenever the left or its allies decide to move against us. It is fairly commonplace for those of us who speak and write frankly about race and equality to encounter audiences where the criticism and hostility of a handful are triumphant, only to find after the speech that we are approached privately by many sympathizers who have sat silent throughout the whole proceeding and said nothing but who now rush to our side to assure us that they really agree with us, only they just can't run the risk of saying so. How sweet. I and Jared Taylor and Phil Rushton and Michael Levin are supposed to run the gauntlet, risk our own jobs and even our physical safety, while others secretly and silently–and safely–applaud.

If you agree with the ideas you have heard at this conference and which you read in *American Renaissance* or in the books by the distinguished authors who have come here and if you believe those ideas are important, then you are going to have to do something yourself, you are going to have to run risks and take hits–not recklessly but with prudence. If we are not prepared to accept some risks and take some hits, then these ideas will never go anywhere, and those on the left who do have the courage to work and fight for their beliefs are going to win. We all know what their victory would mean, and until we are willing to display the kind of courage that civil rights workers in the South showed, that anti-war protesters in the 1960s showed, that indeed "gay rights" activists have shown, until we are willing to risk some of our own security and advantages for what we believe in and for what we believe is fundamental for the survival of our civilization, then we will have no reason for optimism and every reason to expect the victory of our enemies and their lies.

Thank you.

1. Roger Pearson, *Race, Intelligence and Bias in Academe* (Washington , D.C.: Scott-Townsend Publishers, 1991), pp. 283-84.
2. *Ibid.*, p. 225.
3. Kevin P. Phillips, *Mediacracy: American Parties and Politics in the Communications Age* (Garden City, N.Y.: Doubleday & Company, 1975), pp. 32-33.

Cℬℰⴄ

CRSO

Race and Nation

Jared Taylor

I would like to talk to you today about the demographic future of the United States, specifically about what the shifting racial makeup means for the future of our country.

In March, 1996, the Census Bureau released its periodic projection of the ethnic makeup of the United States during the next few decades. It reported that if current immigration and birth rates hold steady, by the year 2050 the percentage of Hispanics will have increased from 10 to 25 percent, Asians from three to eight percent, and blacks from 12 to 14 percent. All these increases will come at the expense of whites, who are projected to fall from 74 percent to about 50 percent.

Within 54 years, therefore, whites will be on the brink of becoming just one more racial minority. And because whites are having so few children, they will be an *old* minority. Within just 34 years they will already account for less than half the population under age 18, but will be three quarters of the population over 65. Many people in this room will be alive to see these things happen.

As usual, the Census Bureau's projections didn't stir much interest, but let us be frank: If this demographic shift takes place it will transform America. It will transform America because race makes a difference. Race matters.

Predictions are usually tricky but when it comes to this transformation, there are a number of things we can say with complete confidence. To know what the future will be like, just visit those cities where the transformation has already taken place–places like Miami or Detroit or Monterey Park, California.

The details of what happens when the population shifts from white to non-white are interesting, but let us set them aside for a moment and consider something else that is profoundly important–something that everyone knows but rarely says–and that is this: Once the number of non-whites in an area reaches a certain level, whites cannot or will not stay. They refuse to be a minority; they move to some other place where they are once again the majority. This is an empirical, utterly dependable fact and everyone–I mean everyone–knows it.

The process never works the other way. Not even the most ardent integrationists are willing to take the obvious, simplest first step to make integration happen, which is to buy a house in a black neighborhood. Or move into a Mexican neighborhood. Or, in many cases, even to send their children to public school.

As far as whites are concerned, once a school or part of a city goes black or Hispanic or sometimes even Asian, it might as well have disappeared from the map. It becomes terra incognita, like those parts of ancient maps that say "Here be dragons." What was once part of American civilization slips its leash and is lost.

Therefore, one certain effect of demographic change will be that whites will withdraw from more and more parts of the United States. It will be *physically possible* for them to live with the Mexicans of Brownsville, Texas, or the blacks of Camden, New Jersey, but whites will go to great lengths to avoid it. After all, whites can think of dozens of places where they would like to live–and they are all likely to have large white majorities. By the same token, most whites cannot name a single majority non-white neighborhood in which they would like to live.

Immigration

Of course, much of the racial shift the Census Bureau predicts would be caused by Third-World immigration. Every year about 800,000 legal immigrants and who-knows-how-many illegal immigrants come to live in this country. Ninety percent of them are non-white. Immigration, however, is not a force of nature. It is the result of a national policy, which Congress could change. By increasing the number of non-white residents, the United States has chosen, in effect, to make more and more parts of itself unappealing to whites.

One often hears that today's non-white immigrants will assimilate just as the European ethnics did at the turn of the century. This view is wrong, because it avoids the fundamental question of race. Germans, Swedes, Poles, Italians and the Irish have assimilated. Blacks and American Indians have been here since colonial times but many are still at the margins of society. Why? Because race largely governs assimilation. Certainly, some non-whites fully embrace European civilization but large numbers do not. Why should they? Their loyalty is, quite naturally, to their own people and their own culture.

Part of today's orthodoxy holds that the reason whites move out of changing neighborhoods is because whites are uniquely racist. I will return to this alleged characteristic of whites, but for now it is worth noting that other races are not keen on living with each other, either.

There are now plenty of places in America where blacks and Hispanics make up most of the public school population. They have race riots and race rivalries in which whites play no part. From Manhattan to Texas to California, high schools and even junior high schools are sometimes shut down because of black versus Hispanic violence and tension.

Likewise, there are prison blocks in Texas and California that are in a constant state of lock down because whenever the prisoners are allowed to leave their cells the blacks and Hispanics go at each others' throats. Racial segregation would, of course, solve this problem but no one dares propose it.

As far as black-Hispanic relations are concerned, I was particularly interested to read the remarks of the president of a black home-owners association in Los Angeles about why she didn't want Mexicans moving into her neighborhood. In 1991, she said to reporters: "It's a different culture, a different breed of people. They don't have the same values. You can't get together with them. It's like mixing oil and water." I sympathize 100 percent with that black lady. Race matters. When the now long-forgotten whites moved out of South-Central Los Angeles, perhaps they said similar things about blacks.

What happens when Asians arrive in large numbers? Their effect is different from that of blacks or Hispanics. Some North Asians commit fewer crimes than whites, make more money, and do better in school. Then there are others, like the Hmong from Cambodia, 60 percent of whom are on welfare. However–and this is a point I wish to emphasize–*it doesn't matter* whether Japanese or Chinese build societies that are, in some respects, objectively superior to those of Europeans. It matters only that they are *different*.

When large numbers of North Asian immigrants moved into Monterey Park, California, whites didn't leave because the newcomers were rioting, or opening crack houses. They moved because Monterey Park, in countless ways, simply ceased to be the town they had grown up in or the town they had moved to. They didn't care that these Asians probably had IQs higher than their own, were responsible parents, and were law-abiding people. Whites saw their way of life melting away beneath their feet, and they moved away in the hope of finding it again elsewhere.

Once again, the particulars of what happens don't matter. It is unwelcome, irreversible racial change that matters.

One significant sign of the times is what is happening on college campuses all around the country. Today's young people have been reared in the most relentlessly anti-racist atmosphere in the history of the world. Over and over they have been told that everybody's beautiful, that distinctions don't matter, that diversity is wonderful, etc. And what do they do as soon as they arrive on campus? They sort themselves out by race. They segregate themselves in social clubs, ethnic dormitories, and all kinds of student activity groups that are defined by race. Race matters, and no amount of propaganda can make it cease to matter.

What will demographic change be like at the national level? That's harder to say. A white majority has already established laws and regulations that discriminate against whites. Many non-whites have convinced themselves that this is equal treatment. If non-whites become the majority, I suspect they will have no trouble convincing themselves that equal treatment calls for yet more preferential measures.

Besides that, what sort of foreign policy would a non-white America have? What would it do–or not do–with nuclear weapons? What sort of government would it have? In the long term, one cannot be sure a non-white America would maintain democracy or the rule of law. The record of non-white nations is not encouraging in this respect.

Even if our forms of government survive, what fanciful readings of the Constitution will emerge from a Supreme Court on which people like Lani Guinier are justices? I suspect that in a non-white America, the First Amendment would go the way of the Tenth, and dissent from racial orthodoxy would be a criminal offense–that it would be impossible to hold a meeting like this one.

Displaced by Non-whites

But to return to the present, in the United States today, there is not a drop of public sympathy for whites who are being displaced by non-whites. We're all supposed to feel morally superior to anyone who escapes to the suburbs when the neighborhood begins to turn black or Mexican. The theory is that only ignorant bigots do this, but the fact is that people with money never have to face the problem. As someone once put it, the purpose of a college education is to give people the right attitudes about minorities and the means to live as far away from them as possible.

This orthodoxy about racial integration has therefore developed a completely transparent set of hypocrisies. Just about every elected official in America, every talking head on television, every self-righteous editorial writer has chanted the mantra of integration so many times, he can recite it in his sleep. But where do these people live? Where do their children go to school? Whom do they invite to their dinner parties? Whom do they marry and urge their children to marry?

They don't actually live and go to school and socialize with these wonderful black people and wonderful Mexicans and Nigerians and Pakistanis. No, integration is a splendid thing–so splendid that they insist that others should enjoy it while they nobly forego the benefits. This is the smelly little consensus that our country's elites have quietly arrived at. "Integration is our goal–but not for me, and my friends, and my children."

And, in fact, these self-righteous, college-educated, properly socialized folks have come up with a whole set of mental exercises for ordinary Americans who don't have the money to live in the suburbs or send their children to private school. The first exercise is to believe that aliens and strangers are bearers of a special gift called diversity. We are not being displaced; we are being enriched and strengthened.

Of course, the idea that racial diversity is a strength is so obviously stupid that only very intelligent people could have thought it up. There is not one multi-racial anything in America that doesn't suffer from racial friction. Our country has established a gigantic, convoluted system of laws, diversity commissions, racial watchdog groups, EEO officers, and outreach committees as part of a huge, clanking mechanism to regulate and try to control racial diversity–something that was supposed to be a great source of strength but that has turned out to be horribly volatile and difficult to manage. People are so exhausted by this alleged source of strength that they run from it the first chance they get. That is why families, churches, clubs, and private parties–which are not yet regulated by the government–are so racially homogeneous.

Nothing, therefore, could be more obvious: Diversity of race or tribe or language or religion are the main reasons people are killing each other all around the world. Just pick up a newspaper. Diversity–within the same territory–is strife, not strength.

Another implausible idea is that a "diverse" workforce is somehow a great advantage for business or world trade. In fact, ninety-nine percent of the things we buy have nothing to do with "diversity." No one cares who makes your shoes or bakes your bread.

And it doesn't take an Irishman to sell things to the Irish. The world's most successful exporting nations are Japan, Korea, Taiwan, and even China, none of which has ever heard of "diversity." American companies are full of blather about how their workforces that "look like America" are going to whip the world–and they are constantly being whipped in their own markets by companies with workforces that look like Yokohama. Diversity a strength? It would be hard to think of anything more obviously untrue.

At the same time, people are so dazed by this incomprehensible diversity argument that they don't seem to notice that only whites apparently suffer from the awful paralysis of homogeneity and have to be gingered up with doses of diversity. No one is urging Howard University, which is overwhelmingly black, to recruit Hispanics or Asians so its students can benefit from racial diversity. No one is saying Mexico must start an immigration program that will reduce Hispanics to a minority in a few decades. But if racial diversity is such a good thing for the United States, why not for Mexico? Why not for Howard University? Why not China or Korea or Tanzania?

Of course, if white Americans were pouring across the border into Mexico demanding that their children be educated in English, insisting on welfare, demanding ballot papers in English rather than Spanish, demanding voting rights for aliens, celebrating July 4th rather than Cinco de Mayo, could anyone trick the Mexicans into thinking this was cultural diversity that should be celebrated? No. The Mexicans would recognize an invasion when they saw one.

"Racial diversity," therefore, is a one-way street. Only whites are ever expected to practice it or benefit from it. The ultimate insult is to expect whites to *celebrate* diversity. This is nothing less than asking them to rejoice in their own capitulation–their dwindling numbers and declining influence. And the astonishing thing is that so many whites have been browbeaten into at least pretending to be happy about this.

For just how long are we supposed to go on cheering our own dispossession? Until we are 49 percent of the population? 25 percent? May we then begin to wonder if this isn't in our interests? Or are we supposed to keep dancing and singing over our own graves until we disappear completely?

The same process of dispossession is at work in Europe, Australia, Canada, and New Zealand. The racial picture is always the same. Whites have built successful, desirable societies–the most successful and desirable in the history of the world. Desperate people from failed, non-white societies are willing to risk nearly everything–sometimes even their lives–for a chance to live in these societies.

But this means that whites face a unique crisis. They are only about fifteen percent of the world's population and are having only about seven percent of the babies. If they let non-whites continue to move into their countries, they will be swept away. Failure to act will ensure oblivion. No other racial group faces this prospect.

Actually Japan, Korea and Taiwan *would* face similar crises if they were governed by the same liberal thinking we permit to govern us. There are millions of Bangladeshis, Malays, and Iraqis who would love to move to Japan for exactly the same reasons Mexicans want to move here, but the Japanese are having none of it. They have the quaint view that Japan should remain Japanese. They like the place the way it is, and know very well that a few million Bangladeshis later, Osaka would no longer be part of Japan.

To repeat, whites and north Asians build successful societies that other races cannot build. That is why non-whites want to come. Nicaraguans and Haitians don't come here out of generosity, eager to share the gift of "diversity" with poor, benighted white people who are about to choke to death on their own homogeneity. They come because their societies don't work and they know life is better here.

If Europeans had turned North America into a giant pesthole no one would want to come. No one would then have to think up elaborate reasons why everyone had the right to come, or why whites actually benefit from being outnumbered and pushed aside by people unlike themselves.

The same process, the same migratory dynamic is at work on a smaller scale. Virtually every desirable place to live, work, or go to school in the United States is desirable because–to put it bluntly–whites made it that way. Non-whites, who do not make things desirable in the same way, want in. This is why it is always non-whites who are pushing their ways into white institutions–never the other way around–and why all the agonizing dramas of "exclusion," "tolerance," "justice," and "racism" are always played out on white territory and put whites on the defensive.

Whites are not clamoring to get into Howard University or live in South Central Los Angeles or move to Guatemala. But if there were something rare and desirable in those places, and non-whites had made them rare and desirable, we can be sure that the proprietors would fight to keep others–including whites–out.

Of course, generally speaking, once non-whites have gotten what they want, and have arrived in large numbers in what were previously white institutions or neighborhoods, those institutions and neighborhoods begin to lose the qualities that made them desirable and attracted non-whites in the first place. Whites leave, and we are right back where

we started. In many respects, blacks and Third-World immigrants rec-
reate in their new locations the places they left behind–complete with
all the shortcomings that prompted them to leave in the first place.

The Message of White Flight

Now, so far, I have not said anything that everyone in America, at
some level, doesn't already know. No school or neighborhood has improved by going from white to black or Hispanic, and whites do not
wait to see whether this time, in their own neighborhoods, something
different is going to happen.

What is the message of all this white flight? It is, quite simply, that
the deepest underlying assumption about race that has directed American policies for the last 40 or 50 years is wrong. The theory–almost
always unstated–was that if we work at it hard enough race can be
made not to matter. This was something that many people thought noble and idealistic, but it was a misreading of human nature. Race matters. It is a brute, biological fact and wishing will not make it go away.

This idea of trying to build a society where race can be made not to
matter reminds me of a different idea that some people thought was
noble and idealistic but that also failed: the idea that people can be
made to live from each according to his ability to each according to his
need. Communism, just like multi-racialism, was founded on a catastrophic misreading of human nature. It staggered on for 75 years, just
as our doomed experiment has staggered on for nearly 50 years, before
it foundered on the simple and obvious fact that people tend their private vegetable gardens more carefully than they work a collective farm.

Of course, communism became a secular religion, just like the doctrine of the unimportance of race has become a secular religion. Both
have their dogmas, their hysterical reactions to dissidents, an astonishing ability to ignore the obvious, their suppression of all disagreement,
their excommunication of heretics. The most remarkable thing, though,
is that whereas it took a government apparatus of repression to force
communism on people, in America, every man is his own commissar
and censors his own thoughts. Even as they are moving to the suburbs,
whites keep insisting that race has nothing to do with it–and many may
actually believe what they are saying. Their orthodoxy requires this.

Of course, an orthodoxy that goes against human nature will eventually collapse just as communism did. The Roman poet Horace explained this more than 2,000 years ago: "You may drive out Nature
with a pitchfork, but she will always return."

Why Have Whites Capitulated?

At some point, nature will reassert itself, and whites will decide not to let themselves be pushed aside. But in the meantime, the real question is why are whites letting this happen to their country. Why do they still pay lip service to ideals of integration that they, themselves, consistently violate? Why are they ensuring that their children and grandchildren will be racial minorities–perhaps even hated minorities–in their own land?

My answer is admittedly speculative, but the reason, I believe, has to do with the perversion of something that is good and characteristic of whites, and that is their sense of reciprocity, of morality. When one thinks of the unique characteristics of Western Civilization that set it off from other civilizations, many boil down to a rooted conviction that can be expressed in very simple terms: That the other fellow has a point of view.

Democracy, for example, is based on the truly heroic proposition that not only does the other fellow have a point of view, but that he is theoretically just as likely to be right as I am. For the most part, only whites have been able to make democracy work. The rule of law is likewise based on the same assumption–that power is not self-justifying, and that the other fellow has a point of view.

European culture is suffused with this notion. The ideals of sportsmanship are designed to ensure fair play and to prevent humiliation of the loser. Freedom of speech and press ensure that the other fellow can express his point of view. The elimination of hereditary class status lets the other fellow rise or fall on his own merits. It was Europeans and Americans who pioneered and perfected these things–much of the rest of the world has yet to come close.

The missionary impulse is also a uniquely European and American undertaking. It's fashionable to laugh at missionaries, but they were driven by a deep concern for the salvation of others. The other fellow not only had a point of view, he had an eternal soul that was in danger of damnation.

The role of women in Western societies reflects the same assumption, except that it is the other sex that has a point of view. Africans and American Indians essentially made women into beasts of burden. Islamic societies kept women indoors or threw blankets over them when they let them out. In Japan, as a Japanese friend once told me, the status of a woman is somewhere between that of a man and a bird. Only in the

West was the weaker sex actually elevated through a code of chivalry and gallantry. The other sex, like the other fellow has a point of view.

Concern for the environment or for wildlife is not universal, either. On this planet, this is an almost exclusively white preoccupation, and it is, in effect, recognition that the other fellow who is not yet even born has a point of view. Some would argue that environmentalism is simply a reflection of the wealth that permits this kind of preoccupation, and to some extent it is.

But what about the Japanese? They are as rich as we are, but when it comes to wildlife, they don't care about saving whales–they'd rather eat them. The Hong Kong Chinese, many of whom could buy or sell Donald Trump if they wanted to, don't care what happens to rhinoceroses or bears, so long as they get their dose of rhino horn or their plate of bear paws. Whites, therefore, take reciprocity and morality to an unusual length; not only does the other fellow have a point of view, the other species has a point of view.

According to orthodoxy whites are, of course, uniquely evil, and certainly not very concerned about the other fellow's point of view. And, indeed, whites have done a lot of killing, particularly in this century. However, the scale of their killing merely reflected their technology. Far more remarkable than the things whites have done is what they have *not* done. They could have kept non-whites in slavery but freed them for moral reasons. For the same reasons they forced non-white peoples to free their own slaves. Whites had the power to colonize the entire world but voluntarily dismantled their empires. Whites still have the power to establish a purely exploitative regimen for the non-white world, but they do not–because the other fellow has a point of view.

Not only does the other fellow have a point of view, this way of thinking has been perverted by current racial orthodoxy to imply that every point of view expressed by non-whites is somehow *superior* to any expressed by whites. When faced with an explicitly racial demand from any non-white group, whites are terrified and demoralized and have lost the argument before it even begins. Robert Frost used to define a liberal is someone who can't take his own side in an argument. Today, whites cannot or dare not take their own side in any kind of racial discussion. They feel they are not even allowed to have a side.

I think, therefore, that the reason whites are paralyzed in the face of national, cultural and racial dispossession is because they are convinced that it would be immoral to resist. Respect for the other fellow's point of view requires that we do nothing to prevent the country from turning into a colony of the Third World. It is the same impulse that makes whites want to save the snail darter and the spotted owl, or to protect the ozone layer, or believe so fervently in democracy–it is this impulse that prevents whites from acting in their own legitimate group interests.

White people reveal what they really think about race, immigration, and the future of their country every time they move to the suburbs. In their bones they know that it will be a calamity if America begins to look (and act) exactly like those places where whites refuse to live. Whites are deeply, deeply pessimistic and very much afraid of a non-white future for their children. But they dare not say so. They have convinced themselves that to speak would be immoral, that nothing is worse than to open themselves to the charge of racism.

I believe that this is a perversion of what is in fact one of the hallmarks of Western man–his abiding sense of reciprocity. However, when every other race is conscious of its racial interests and works diligently to advance them, any race that does not has committed unilateral disarmament in a dangerous world.

The moral question can be put this way. Let us imagine that Mexico invaded and conquered the south-eastern part of the United States. What would the Mexicans do with their new territory? They would establish Spanish as the official language. They would expel much of the white population and replace it with Mexicans. They would abolish American holidays and celebrate Mexican ones. Music, food, education, work habits, religion, primary loyalties, and the very texture of life–all would become Mexican rather than American.

Of course, as I suggested earlier, this is exactly what has already happened in many parts of California and Texas. And a similar invasion from Central America has, in 30 years, reduced the percentage of whites in Miami from 90 percent to 10 percent. Ninety percent to 10 percent in just 30 years! Likewise, the inner cities of our great metropolises have, in effect, been taken over by Liberia.

Those parts of the country are lost to Euro-American culture and even nationality. America has therefore given up the very thing nations go to war to preserve, the very thing they send their young men into battle to die for. The integrity of a people, race, or nation is so important that sometimes millions of men are sacrificed in their name. Why? Because the preservation of the nation of one's forefathers is more important than life itself.

Obviously, it would be moral to stop an armed invasion by Mexico. Why is it wrong to resist an unarmed process that produces the same results? Why is it wrong to take peaceful measures to forestall the catastrophe that nations wage all-out war in order to prevent?

Before he was assassinated, Yitzhak Rabin explained that what mattered most to him as an Israeli was that Israel remain at least 80 percent Jewish. So far as I know, no one called Mr. Rabin a hatemonger or a bigot. But we know what would be said about any white politician who advocated that America stay at least 80 percent white. And yet, the reasoning and morality of an American white and an Israeli Jew, are identical. Israel will change in countless, unacceptable ways if it ceases to be Jewish, just as America will change in countless unacceptable ways if it ceases to be white.

The forms of civility, the folkways, the demeanor and the texture of life that whites take for granted cannot survive the embrace of large numbers of aliens. The things that I love most about culture and human society have not survived in Detroit and Miami. That is why whites have left. It may not be "nice" to say these things. But for fear of being thought not "nice" whites are preparing to leave to their grandchildren a Third-World nation. I can scarcely think of a greater act of collective cowardice and irresponsibility.

Americans have known for hundreds of years that multi-racialism of the kind we are supposed to be practicing today would be disastrous. You may recall the American Colonization Society. Its purpose was to free blacks from slavery and persuade them to go to Africa. A list of some of its officers–and these were *officers*, not just supporters–reads like an honor roll from American history: James Madison, Andrew Jackson, Daniel Webster, Stephen Douglas, William Seward, Francis Scott Key, General Winfield Scott, two Chief Justices of the U.S. Supreme Court: John Marshall and Roger Taney.

The Liberians named their capital Monrovia, in recognition of James Monroe's efforts to encourage colonization. Abraham Lincoln and Thomas Jefferson also favored colonization; both believed it was impossible for blacks and whites to live together as free men in the same society.

The intellectual antecedents for racial disengagement therefore include many of the genuinely great men of our past. The current fad of multi-racialism is only a few decades old. Not one great American ever advocated it. Presumably, we are supposed to believe that Jefferson and Lincoln and John Marshall were great men, but when it came to race they somehow got it wrong. Well, who got it right? Ted Kennedy? Bill Clinton?

In conclusion, the Americans of the past would look with horror upon what we are doing. I am quite certain that my ancestors did not fight for independence from Britain in order for our generation to turn the country over to Mexicans and Haitians. The Founders did not frame the Constitution to celebrate diversity. Americans did not spill their blood at Gettysburg or in Europe or the Pacific for multiculturalism. And yet, we are giving up our country without a struggle.

What we are witnessing is one of the great tragedies in human history. Powerful forces are in motion that, if left unchecked, will slowly push aside European man and European civilization on this continent. If we do nothing, the nation we leave to our grandchildren will be a grim, Third-World failure, in which whites will be a minority. Western Civilization will be a faint echo, probably vilified if it is even audible. I cannot think of a tragedy that is at once so great, so unnatural, and so unnecessary.

Cℨ℠

Immigration, Sovereignty, and the Future of the West

Wayne Lutton

The topic on which I have been invited to speak–immigration–is probably the least "controversial" of all the issues dealt with at this conference. While there has been a sustained effort to try to prevent a public debate about this subject, a clear majority of American adults are opposed to the sort of immigration policies that have been in effect here since the impact of the 1965 Immigration Act became clear. Unlike abortion, welfare reform, gun control, balancing the federal budget, or other current issues, immigration policy is not a contentious question. However, there is clearly a gap between public sentiment and public policy in this area.

The Roper poll released at the end of February, 1996, revealed a consensus against high levels of immigration:

• Eighty-three percent of Americans favored a lower level of immigration than the current average of over a million a year.

• Some 70 percent wanted fewer than 300,000 immigrants per year. This view was endorsed by 52 percent of Hispanics, 73 percent of blacks, 72 percent of conservatives, 71 percent of moderates, 66 percent of liberals, 72 percent of Democrats, and 70 percent of Republicans.

• A majority supported even larger cuts, with 54 percent agreeing that annual immigration should be less than 100,000. The *Wall Street Journal* noted in March, 1996, that a majority of American adults now support a five-year moratorium on all legal immigration. The Roper poll I've been referring to found that over a fifth of Americans want no more immigration at all.

As for illegal immigration, the Roper organization found that strong measures to halt it are favored by 78 percent of self-styled moderates, 76 percent of the strongly religious, 77 percent of whites, 82 percent of Protestants, 85 percent of Midwesterners, 60 percent of English-speaking Hispanics, 68 percent of blacks, and 69 percent of Catholics.

The latest results confirm what several decades of polling on the subject have consistently shown, namely, that a majority of the public has never supported the immigration policies enacted by Congress and the Executive Branch.

Opening the Gates

Polling done in Australia, New Zealand, and Canada shows a similar gap between public sentiment and public policy. It is more than merely noteworthy that in addition to the United States these countries are the only ones that today admit large numbers of legal immigrants. They were, at least until recently, the most successful outposts of British colonization.

All four countries opened their doors to large-scale Third World immigration at just about the same time: the U.S. and Canada in the mid-1960s, and Australia and New Zealand by the early 1970s.

In the case of the United States, we have endured over 30 years of uninterrupted mass immigration, with legal immigration averaging around a million people annually, in addition to the hundreds of thousands of illegal immigrants permitted to settle here every year.

As we all know, prior to the 1965 Immigration Act, the United States was bedeviled with the problems associated with the presence in our midst of a large population descended from natives of sub-Saharan Africa. Since the passage of the 1965 Immigration Act, followed by the 1980 Refugee Act, the 1986 Immigration Reform & Control Act (which did neither), and the 1990 Immigration Act (which raised legal immigration by nearly 40 percent) America's racial problems have only multiplied.

Even before passage of the 1965 Immigration Act, the Kennedy administration took steps to increase immigration from non-European countries by granting quotas to newly independent Aisan, Caribbean, and African nations. Kennedy also relaxed restrictions against the admission of aliens afflicted with various contagious diseases, including leprosy and tuberculosis. His administration also sponsored the 1962 Migration & Refugee Act, which gave authority to the United Nations High Commissioner for Refugees to determine the status of refugees, some of whom were then to be admitted to the U.S. Our government deliberately surrendered its rights to define the criteria upon which a certain class of immigrants would be admitted.

Doris Meissner, President Bill Clinton's commissioner of the Immigration & Naturalization Service (INS), has boasted that "we are transforming ourselves." No truer words have been spoken by any Clinton administration official. Over 90 percent of legal and well over 90 percent of illegal immigrants are Third World natives. For 1995, the top ten countries of birth for legal immigrants were, in the following order:

Mexico
Philippines
Vietnam
Dominican Republic
Mainland China
India
Cuba
Ukraine
Jamaica
Korea

In 1965 there were some 800,000 Asians living in the United States. Over the past quarter-century, some 5.6 million have been allowed to immigrate, which is about 1,100 times more than Senator Robert Kennedy predicted would arrive after passage of the 1965 Immigration Act (he testified that "a maximum" of 5,000 Asians would migrate to the U.S. annually). Including the children of recent Asian immigrants, the Asian population has grown to eight million. Hundreds of thousands more have settled in Canada, New Zealand, and Australia.

The Census Bureau reported in March, 1996, that the U.S. had reached a turning point during Fiscal Year 1993-94: The increase in the Hispanic population was greater than that of non-Hispanic whites. This was the first time whites have trailed another group, at least since the 18th century. Census Bureau figures indicate that non-Hispanic whites— the people who used to be referred to as "Americans"–constituted 88 percent of the population in 1960. Thirty years later they had been reduced to 73 percent. By 1990, proportionally, there were fewer European Americans than in 1790.

If trends continue, it is projected that European Americans will be a numerical minority in California in seven years, and in what was once the United States, as a whole, within sixty years.

Internal Migration

Many Americans have quietly packed up and fled the regions where the impact of immigration is greatest. Some have migrated to Washington state and Oregon. Others are moving to the Rocky Mountain region, or elsewhere into the interior, or to such states as Maine, New Hampshire, and Vermont that still have large white populations. Demographer William Frey of the University of Michigan has been following this internal migration, and notes that some areas are becoming more homogenous as millions of Americans choose to escape from "diversity." Whites are not the only ones exiting areas of heavy immigrant settlement; many American blacks are leaving too, with the South being the destination of preference for large numbers.

Those who stay behind are increasingly huddling inside walled and gated communities, which have been springing up in coastal areas, especially in California, Texas, and Florida. This follows the abandonment of our cities by the white majority, sparked by forced integration of public schools in the early 1960s, and which accelerated after the race riots of the mid-to-late 1960s. To my knowledge, never before in history has a majority population simply picked up and left behind the equivalent of trillions of dollars worth of infrastructure, homes, museums and other public facilities, which they have then had to rebuild in new communities.

Problems Associated With Immigration

It is no wonder that the American public has grown increasingly troubled about immigration policy. This unease is well founded; immigration, both legal and illegal, is contributing to a host of national problems.

• Impact on Jobs: We now admit as many or more people than the net number of new jobs created every year in the economy. In 1996, 3.5 million Americans turned 18. The Labor Department projected that around 1.2 million net new jobs would open. In addition, a million legal immigrants and several hundred thousand illegal immigrants were likely to be admitted.

In 1995, in the area of professional employment, the software industry needed about 40,000 new workers–far fewer than the 51,000 new computer science graduates leaving our universities. Yet the number of foreign computer programmers granted work visas exceeded 30,000. Prof. Norman Matloff of the University of California at Davis reminds us that only 1 out of 56 recipients of the computer industry awards for technological advance have gone to immigrants. All the rest have gone to U.S. natives, giving the lie to the view that immigration is necessary for innovation. Silicon Valley wants to hire foreign nationals because they are willing to work for lower salaries in exchange for the chance to live here. Sun Microsystems has publicly admitted that it hires low-salary foreigners.

• Crime: Around a quarter to a third of the federal prison population in any given year is made up of the foreign-born. The FBI reports that 57 percent of the recent increase in juvenile and teen-age crime is accounted for by Hispanics. Foreign criminal syndicates are flourishing, led by Chinese Triads, Japanese Yakuza, Jamaicans, Nigerians, etc. The California Attorney General warns that his state has been invaded by the "Russian" Mafia, (members of which entered the U.S. under the special Jewish refugee admission program.)

Dominican drug lords in New York City are so powerful that they were able to obtain the conviction of Joseph Occhipinti, the head of the INS Organized Crime/Drug Enforcement Task Force in Upper Manhattan, on charges of conducting illegal searches of drug dens operating out of *boedgas* (Hispanic grocery stores). Occhipinti served seven months of a 37-year prison term before President George Bush commuted his sentence. Staten Island Borough President Guy Molinari is convinced that the dedicated INS crime fighter was framed and convicted on the basis of perjured testimony of alien drug dealers.

• Welfare Costs: Welfare use by immigrants is rising, even as it is declining for Americans. Immigrants use welfare at higher rates than native-born Americans, and at much higher rates than white Americans. George Borjas of Harvard University reports in the May 1996 issue of the *Quarterly Journal of Economics* that taking all types of welfare together, immigrants have a 47 percent higher use of such programs–20.7 percent versus 14.1 percent of the U.S. population as a whole. Immigrants are more likely than Americans to participate in practically every means-tested program.

Prof. Borjas reveals that the overall "welfare gap" becomes even wider if immigrants are compared with non-Hispanic, white native-born households, with immigrants being almost twice as likely to receive assistance–20.7 percent versus 10.5 percent. In California, immigrants make up 21 percent of the households, but consume 39.5 percent of the benefit dollars. In Texas, 8.9 percent of the households are immigrants, and receive 22 percent of the benefits. In New York state, immigrants constitute 16 percent of the households and receive an estimated 22.2 percent of the benefits. Not only do immigrants use welfare programs at a higher rate than Americans, but a higher percentage remain on welfare more or less permanently.

Donald Huddle of Rice University estimates that the "immigrant deficit"—what the 24.4 million legal and illegal immigrants who have settled in the United States since 1970 will cost in excess of taxes they paid—is averaging $60 billion per year and growing.

It should be remembered than *any* immigrant welfare usage goes against the intent of immigration laws going back to colonial times, and our first federal immigration laws passed in the 19th century. Those likely to become a "public charge" are not supposed to be admitted.

The Clinton administration recently had the INS define mental, physical, and developmental disabilities as "expanded exemptions" for naturalization applicants. This exempts certain "disabled" persons from the requirements of English literacy and knowledge of United States history if the person is unable to comply because of a physical or mental disability. U.S. citizenship is now to be granted to another class of people who should not be permitted to land on our shores in the first place.

• Environmental degradation: Water tables are dropping in such high-population-growth states as Florida, California, Texas, and Arizona. The benefits of the Clean Air Act have been largely canceled out by immigration-fueled population increases. Wildlife habitats are threatened as never before by a population that is surging—thanks to recent immigrants and their offspring, not to a "baby boom" touched off by pre-1965 Americans.

• Balkanization: This becomes ever more likely, as real Americans flee from parts of what was once their country. In Miami, Florida, for instance, as soon as Hispanics became a majority, they repealed the Official English Amendment that required the use of English in local government documents and procedures. A revived AZTLAN Movement (seeking to establish a new, all-Hispanic nation in the South West) has re-emerged. As the Mexican-American politician and sometime California State Senator Art Torres put it in 1995, Proposition-187 (a California ballot initiative to deny welfare to illegal immigrants) was the "last gasp of White America."

Huddled Masses

The U.S. government has allowed certain Third World countries to export large segments of their populations here. Since the early 1980s, $1/5$ of the population of El Salvador has moved to America, as has $1/6$ of that of Haiti. The government is making sure newcomers feel right at home. In April, 1995, the State Department proposed providing "cultural orientation programs" for Iraqis in the wake of reports about the high incidence of pedophilia and rape committed by recent Iraqi refugees.

Female circumcision (genital mutilation) is practiced here now by immigrants from Africa and the Middle East. Ironically, for those who have not yet come, opposition to this ancient rite is cited as sufficient grounds for admission as a "refugee." Genital mutilation is the custom in some 26 African and Middle Eastern countries. How many natives of these lands will be admitted in the future?

Kidnapping of child-brides, a Laotian prenuptial custom, is now practiced in the United States. A man, often in his thirties, makes off with a girl in her early-to-mid teens, and has sex with her for three days. They are then declared married. However, if, after trying her out for a while, the "husband" decides she is lazy, or is otherwise unhappy with her, the now-violated girl can be returned to her family. The return of a kidnapped bride is considered a great disgrace, and has led anguished Laotians living in the U.S. to commit suicide or kill members of their own families.

"Cultural orientation" is now offered as a defense in criminal cases. In one of the first instances of this newly accepted judicial stance, New York State judge Edward Pincus cited "cultural differences" when he granted Dong Lu Chen probation after the Chinese immigrant beat his 99-pound wife to death with a hammer. Chen claimed his anger was justified because his wife had been unfaithful.

In a 1996 case in La Crosse, Wisconsin, Judge Ramona Gonzalez sentenced a Southeast Asian immigrant, Sia Ye Vang, 32, to take English lessons (in addition to probation and community service) instead of going to prison, after he was convicted of molesting his two stepdaughters, aged 10 and 11. Yang's lawyer, Katherine Schnell, argued that sex with young girls is an accepted part of Asian culture. Judge Gonzalez said that she wanted to allow Vang "the opportunity to continue his education and his assimilation into our culture." (That Wisconsin, a state settled by Germans and Scandinavians, is now blessed with a Judge Gonzalez, is itself a sign of worrisome demographic shift.)

In the summer of 1996, San Francisco Deputy District Attorney Susan Breall, dropped statutory rape charges against Iraqi native Mohammed Alsreafi, aged 30, who had sex with an 11-year-old girl. Breall told the *San Francisco Chronicle* that she did not want to be accused of putting his culture on trial when "I and many other San Franciscans pride ourselves on being sensitive to someone's culture."

That pre-modern people engage in practices Westerners find odd, repellent, or illegal is nothing new. What is remarkable is that we allow people who indulge in such practices to be imported by the million into our country. What we are witnessing is the creation of a new doctrine: that the alleged needs of people bred to other norms give them the right to violate ours.

Culture Clash–The Spread of Witchcraft in America

George Bush's Vice President, Dan Quayle, was one of the many cheerleaders for multiculturalism, who took pride in declaring at every opportunity that "our strength is in our diversity."

One variety of "diversity" the new immigration has brought is witchcraft. In parts of the former United States boasting populations from Mexico, Central America, the Caribbean, and Africa, stores catering to the followers of all manner of dark cults can be found in nearly every neighborhood. In cities with large Hispanic populations, such as Miami, Houston, Los Angeles, New York, and Chicago, there are areas where *botanicas* can be found two or three to a block. These are stores that cater to superstitions and carry everything needed to cast a spell, remove a hex, or heal a physical or mental disorder. Shelves are stocked with Haitian voodoo dolls, crucifixes, protective amulets, medicinal herbs, incense, and votive candles to summon or give thanks to the deity of your choice. *Botanicas* also sell statues of Catholic saints for practitioners of Santeria, Palo Mayombe, Brujereia, or Macumba, Umbanda, Candomble, and other voodoo-like cults especially popular in Brazil.

Casting spells and hexes has become an increasingly familiar part of the criminal justice system in our ever-more "diverse" America. In 1995, it was widely reported that the Dade County (Greater Miami), Florida courthouse is littered with dead animals, offered as ritual sacrifices by members of Miami's large Caribbean immigrant population. Dead chickens, goat heads, and lizards with their mouths tied shut–a none too subtle message to witnesses and informers–are swept up daily by maintenance workers, who have been dubbed the "Voodoo Squad." Court houses in other cities in Florida, New York, California, Texas, and other centers of Hispanic and African settlement report the same thing.

Santeria is a gruesome Afro-Caribbean religion that is essentially a version of Haitian voodoo brought over to the U.S.A. by Cubans in the early 1960s. In its present form, it was first practiced around 2,500 BC in what is now Nigeria. Yoruba tribesmen developed a nature religion that allowed mortals to approach gods through the worship of natural objects, such as shells, feathers, and herbs.

Santeria–Spanish for "worship of saints"–spread to the New World in the 1500s. African slaves substituted their own gods for Catholic saints. They might bow down to Saint Lazarus, but direct their prayers to Babalu-Aye, the Yoruba god and patron of the sick. When they kneeled before Christ on the cross, they may have been calling on Oloru'n Orofi, the great Creator. Santeria established an especially strong presence in Cuba and Brazil, where, in slightly different form, it is known as Macumba or Umbanda.

Today, Santeria practitioners are known as Santeros, and they worship a bewildering array of deities, called orishas, who are represented in their dual role as Catholic saints and ancient African gods. Santeros believe that every person is assigned a particular orisha at birth, which acts as a guardian angel of sorts. The believer also has his own special plant, animal, and birthstone but he must discover which orisha has been assigned to him. If you can discover your orisha, you can improve your fortune by always carrying your specific orisha symbols with you.

While the Christian god is believed to be loving, generous, and helpful to those who honor and pray to Him, followers of Santeria and the other cults I have mentioned believe that malevolent deities must constantly be appeased with offerings. Common to these sects is belief in the power of blood sacrifice, which gives the orishas something in return for their helpful magic. Goats and chickens are the animals most often sacrificed. Drug dealers, alien smugglers, and other criminal elements are particularly given to appealing to spirits for enrichment and for protection from the hated "Anglos" or business competitors.

In metropolitan areas that are still inhabited by Americans, nonbelievers have charged Santeros with animal cruelty and have complained to the police about their sacrificial rituals. The city of Hialeah, Florida, went all the way to the Supreme Court in what proved to be an unsuccessful effort to curb these barbaric practices, which were ruled to be protected forms of religion.

The attorney who crossed swords with the Santeros in this case charged that Santeria is little different from Palo Mayombe, many of whose followers hold Oggun–the patron saint of criminals and crime–in the highest esteem. It should be noted that Palo Mayombe enjoys a strong following among the criminals who arrived in the U.S. during the 1980 Mariel boat-lift from Cuba.

In Palo Mayombe rites, animals–and sometimes even humans–are sacrificed after torture and mutilation. Pain and fear are powerful elements of the ritual. The blood of the sacrificial victim is then consumed by participants, as are some of the body parts. Efforts have been made to calm the public–that is, us–by claiming that most followers obtain human organs by robbing graves or medical supply warehouses. However, a number of cases have leaked to the public of actual human sacrifice. Perhaps the most notorious (to date) was the kidnapping of Mark Kilroy, a college student who went to Metamoros, Mexico from Brownsville, Texas with some of his friends during a 1989 Spring Break pub crawl. The blond baseball player and engineering student was abducted and sacrificed by a drug and alien smuggling ring led by an American-born Cuban, Adolfo Jesus Constanzo.

Cultural anthropologists explain that practitioners of Palo Mayombe eat human bones and other body parts (sexual organs are especially prized) because they believe this gives them power. Spirits are believed to live in the bodies of the sacrificial victims and these spirits can be enslaved for future use.

My point in discussing these practices is that they illustrate what has been happening in the United States and other Western countries. People are carriers of and contributors to culture. Non- and anti-Western people, with their colorful, "diverse" practices, should not be made welcome, and their presence in our midst should not be tolerated.

The Question of Sovereignty

For several decades, the concepts of consent, sovereignty, and self-determination have been under assault in Western countries. In the U.S., government agencies and the courts have extended privileges formerly reserved to citizens, such as education, health care, and housing assistance, to aliens whose very presence is against the express wishes of the national community.

The American people are no longer allowed to determine for themselves who will be admitted to their nation. Historically, the determination of who is a citizen has been intrinsic to national self-determination. The concept of citizenship has been the cornerstone of the nation-state. In the United States and other Western nations, the state exists to protect the rights and interests *of its citizens*.

Thanks to the post-World War II emphasis on universal and transnational rights, distinctions between "national" and "alien" are thought to be suspect. The right of aliens to make claims on the citizens of other countries, stated in terms of "international human rights," has played a major role in changing the character of the state and its basis of legitimacy.

The purpose of government, in the West, has been turned on its head. Instead of acting as the representative, and for the benefit, of its own nationals, it is now accountable to international institutions and rules for treating people who happen to be residing within its borders.

The West has therefore witnessed the emergence of transnational rights during an era of renewed transnational migration. Since 1970, U.S. federal courts have cited provisions of the Universal Declaration of Human Rights in cases involving aliens and refugees. And the European Commission on Human Rights has been cited in U.S. courts as a recognized instrument of international human rights law. I need hardly add that this has been used as a further excuse to expand the state bureaucracy to monitor the "rights" of various constituencies–newly favored groups, such as migrants, racial, religious, and "gender" minorities, women, and the physically and mentally handicapped.

In 1996, representatives of the governments of the United States and Canada participated in a Regional Conference on Migration, held in Puebla, Mexico. They solemnly pledged to work against the demands of their own citizens for immigration restriction and control. As the *San Diego Union-Tribune* reported in its March 15, 1996 issue, "The United States, Canada, and eight Latin American nations pledged to defend migrants' rights and protect them from violence, xenophobia and traffickers. In a joint statement at the end of the historic two-day Regional Conference on Migration, participants condemned violations of migrants' human rights and promised to respect their dignity. . . . The Puebla conference concluded that by and large, migration is a beneficial phenomenon with potential advantages for both countries of origin and destination. . . . The ten nations agreed to counteract anti-immigrant attitudes."

As we approach the end of the twentieth century, we see that the state is no longer the embodiment of the "general will" of a particular people or nation–at least not of some peoples and nations. As a practical matter, abandonment of sovereignty is limited to Western Europe, North America, Australia, and New Zealand.

Were we meeting today in Toronto, or London, Paris, Auckland, or Melbourne, my message would be the same. The West is under assault. If we fail to regain control of our nations, of our destinies, our people and the civilization they have created over centuries will disappear.

As we survey the wreckage of what was once the United States, we should be looking *forward*, as Kant invited us to do, when he observed, "There is a kingdom which does not yet exist, but can be realized through our actions."

ⱯⱯ

CR&SO

Recent Fallacies in Discussions of Race

Michael Levin

It is an embarrassment to defenders of the intellectual parity of the races that all the evidence goes against them. Black children fall behind white children in school from the earliest grades. No black society has ever produced a written language or mathematics, while whites and Asians have done so many times. Whites consistently outscore blacks on IQ tests.

Lacking any case *for* racial equality in intelligence, egalitarians are forced to attack the abundant evidence *against* it. This negative, reactive approach encourages far-fetched reinterpretations of data–e.g., blacks do badly on tests because of worry that poor performance will reflect on their race–as well as purely definitional and conceptual objections. Thus, until recently, the favored criticisms of IQ tests were that "intelligence" is meaningless and that the tests are biased. (These criticisms are inconsistent, by the way, since a test for a non-existent trait cannot be biased, that is to say, measure the trait more accurately for one group than another.) The wide publicity given the validity of intelligence testing by Herrnstein and Murray (1994) seems to have lessened carping about IQ per se, at least for now, but egalitarians have simply directed their attacks elsewhere. The present essay looks at some newer but no sounder efforts to discredit inegalitarianism.

I have sorted the fallacies discussed below into the purely verbal, those concerning gene-environment interaction, and those concerning heritability. Other egalitarian arguments the reader is apt to meet will probably fall into one of these categories.

The Purely Verbal

Since it is now widely agreed that "intelligence" names an intrinsic property of the mind, only one purely verbal ploy is currently used by egalitarians, namely the alleged vagueness of "race." No race can be more or less intelligent than any other, we are assured, since there is no such thing as race. Why, allegedly, is there no such thing as race? Because genetic differences between human groups are insignificant, human groups have cross-bred, and given the unlimited number of ways to classify human beings any one classification is arbitrary.

Scientific friends of the concept of race will rush to defend it because of its fruitfulness and predictive validity, but I fear that defense just sustains the imbroglio. Decades of dealing with disputes about "free will," "knowledge" and kindred philosophical terms have convinced me that as soon as someone starts to make heavy weather over a word, one should abandon it. Disavow its use, and then, since the storm was about language rather than facts, restate the facts without it. Your interlocutor should be delighted–he's the one unhappy with the term, after all–although in practice you may find him aggrieved. When people don't want clarity, as Sam Goldwyn might have said, nothing can stop them.* No other tactic really has any chance of moving the debate forward. An invitation to mud-wrestle should not prompt a search for the best hold; the smart move is to stay out of the mud.

The smart move in the present instance is to drop the word "race" and reformulate whatever you wish to say without it. What people usually have in mind by "race" is geographic ancestry, as indicated by the interchangeability of "black" with "African-American," and by liberal indignation at "Eurocentrism" when they really mean to attack whites. Consequently, instead of saying that whites are more intelligent than blacks, say that people of European ancestry are more intelligent than people of sub-Saharan African ancestry. To allow for the intermarriage that has occurred in the U.S. over the past three centuries, refine this to: People of European ancestry are more intelligent than people, 75 percent or more of whose ancestors 10 generations back, were born in sub-Saharan Africa. These paraphrases, using only notions like "ancestor" that even obscurantists accept, engage the substantive issues. Nothing is lost but a word.

Nor do the seemingly small genetic differences between Africans and Europeans nullify talk of ancestry. Cavalli-Sforza, Menozzi and Piazza (1994) report that the typical European and African share 99.84 percent of their genes. But one cannot reason a priori that an absolute

---

* Block and Dworkin (1976) complain at length about the uselessness of the word "intelligence," but then criticize Arthur Jensen for jettisoning the word in favor of a psychometric substitute.

difference of 0.0016 percent is too small to support genetic divergence in IQ. Genetic effects tend to be nonlinear; even minute genetic differences can bear large phenotypic consequences.[*] Humans and chimpanzees have 98.4 percent of their genes in common. (This is so simply because most human and chimp genes are dedicated to building hearts, lungs and other shared gross structures). This does not make chimpanzees as intelligent as humans. The human/gorilla genetic difference, at 2.5 percent (Caccone and Powell 1989), is 1.5 times the human-chimp difference, but the human/gorilla IQ gap is not 1.5 times the human/chimp gap. It would not be surprising if world-class golfers differ from the average duffer in the genes controlling coordination by less than 0.0016 percent. One must *first* determine the contribution of a genetic difference to phenotypic differences, individual or group, and *then* decide whether it is "significant."

Incidentally, Cavalli-Sforza, Menozzi and Piazza also report that the average genetic "distance" between humans is 0.0012 percent of the genome,[†] which puts the black/white distance a third again as great as the average, a surplus anything but trivial.

An allied and quite popular statistical fallacy is that within-race genetic variations so exceed between-group differences that talk of group differences is "meaningless" (Gould 1995). This is like arguing that, since the variation in weight among dogs and among cats is greater than the mean dog/cat difference, it is meaningless to say that dogs on average outweigh cats.

Gene-Environment Interaction

Interaction fallacies are inspired by the dependence of a gene's phenotypic expression on the environment in which the gene is situated. A gene may express itself differently in different environments; newborns with identical "growth genes" will reach different heights should one be raised on a balanced diet while the other consumes nothing but Big Macs. Also–by definition–different alleles[‡] for a trait

---

[*] A *phenotype* is any trait of an organism; height, birth weight, and IQ are all phenotypes. A *genotype* is the genetic basis of observed traits.

[†] The *genome* is the totality of human genes.

[‡] Phenotypes are controlled by the genes at particular locations on chromosomes. Several different genes may occupy the locus controlling height, for example, and each of these different "genes for height" is called an allele.

may express themselves differently in the same environment (this is the technical definition of "interaction") *and* the difference in the phenotypic expressions of two genes may itself vary from one environment to another. A Tutsi child might grow no taller than an Eskimo child if both were enclosed from birth in tiny suits of armor that did not permit growth.

Where environmentalists go wrong is in inferring from the dependence of phenotypes on environment that genes are irrelevant to phenotypic outcomes, and that any phenotypic outcome can be attained by environmental manipulation. From this it is concluded–by Jencks (1992), Layzer (1973), Baumrind (1991), Root (1993),[*] Lewontin (1976a, 1976b, 1976c), Block (1995), Goldberger and Manski (1995) and many others–that individual and group IQs are not decrees of nature but human choices. Lewontin (1970) asserts confidently that "we" [unspecified] can increase IQ "as much or as little as our social values may eventually demand." According to a slightly weaker version of this doctrine, genes in no way constrain attempts to eliminate the race gap by environmental manipulation: "we [again unspecified] should . . . *simply try out new environments* (Block 1995, italics in original).

The obvious error here is that, while genes *may* not dictate individual IQs or group IQ differences, it is also possible that they do. The inference that genes don't matter treats what *might be possible* as if it were *actually true*. Some traits, such as eye color, are fixed. Since no environmental intervention has ever raised anyone's IQ permanently, there is reason to think IQ is likewise fixed. Moreover, even if genes do not rigidly fix IQ or IQ differences, they may still limit what environmental manipulation can achieve. Height is not fixed by genes, but no dietary regimen will produce a man ten feet tall, or make women on average taller than men.

Those who wish to equalize IQs by manipulating the environment stress that a genotype's "reaction range," its expressions over all possible environments, cannot be inferred from its expressions in a finite sample of environments. But reaction ranges don't cover every conceivable phenotypic expression–a height of ten feet is beyond the range of any human genotype–and God has given no guarantee that there are environments in which black and white IQs will be equal.

An ominous twist to this interaction fallacy that occurred to me as a mere hypothetical possibility when writing Levin (1997) has in fact been proposed by Goldberger and Manski (1995). To understand it

---

[*] For sex differences.

please look at Figure 1 on this page, in which curve W represents the reaction range of the average white gene[*] for intelligence, and B represents the reaction range of the average black gene for intelligence.

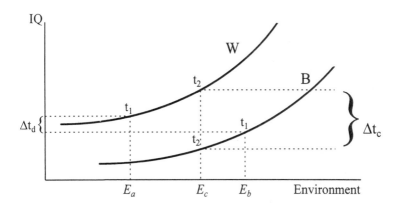

Suppose that in any environment like E_c, which is common to both races, the difference is large; I've called it Δt_c. But suppose as well that some environments, such as E_a, are less favorable to the expression of intelligence than others, such as E_b. The IQ gap can therefore be reduced to the small value Δt_d ('d' for "diverse") by putting whites in the unfavorable E_a and blacks in the favorable E_b. Goldberger and Manski (1995: 764-765) tiptoe up to this proposal in language I will translate into English:

> [A]n individual's observed IQ test score Y is the sum of her "genotype" Z and her "environment" U, so $Y = Z+U$. Imagine that Z and U are uncorrelated, so the variance of Y equals the variance of Z plus the variance of U: $V(Y)+V(U)$. . . [The usual] thought experiment call[s] for equalizing environments, making $V(U) = 0$. Suppose instead that we preserve $V(U)$ at its current value, but make U perfectly negatively correlated with Z by introducing an extreme compensatory policy. The IQ variance would fall from $V(Y)(h^2+e^2)$ to $V(Y)(h^2+e^2-2he)=V(Y)(h-e)^2$. So with $h^2 = 0.6$ and $e^2 = 0.4$, this intervention would reduce IQ variance to $(\sqrt{.6}-\sqrt{.4})^2 = 2$ percent of its current value $V(Y)$.

---

[*] I use "gene for a trait" to mean whatever portion of the DNA affects that trait. It need not be any one small continuous stretch of DNA.

The idea here (couched in nonstandard notation as well as politically correct pronouns) is to go beyond equalization of environments–fairness as usually conceived–and put high-intelligence genotypes in environments that depress them and low-intelligence genotypes in environments that stimulate them. Goldberger and Manski refrain from specifying "extreme" compensation more precisely, but almost any concrete proposal would have to be quite radical. For instance, many commentators blame the IQ gap on the dullness of black households, so "compensation" might mean giving black children to white parents and white children to black parents, or letting white parents keep their children but limiting the reading matter in their homes. Other commentators blame low black IQ on disorderly black neighborhoods, so "compensation" might mean moving black families to the suburbs and white families to the slums. (The problem,[*] of course, is that putting too many whites in Harlem would turn it into Scarsdale, and vice-versa for blacks in Scarsdale.) I expect that as the genetic origin of the racial IQ gap becomes undeniable, i.e., as it becomes clear that the mean white IQ will exceed the mean black IQ in virtually any $common^{\dagger}$ environment, egalitarians will increasingly favor Goldberger-Manski "compensation." White tolerance of such measures might seem unthinkable, but the white elite's enthusiasm for affirmative action leaves the possibility distinctly open.

Environmentalists stress that environmental differentiation can cloak genetic similarity. Blacks only seem genetically inferior in intelligence, the argument goes, because poor environments acting on genes identical to those of whites produce a lower phenotypic IQ. In the terms of Figure 1, W describes both black and white genotypes, but blacks occupy E_a while whites occupy E_b. However, Figure 1 also illustrates how environmental differentiation can cloak genetic *differences*. If W and B are indeed distinct, but W is in E_a and B in E_b (the sort of environmental manipulation that Goldberger-Manski hint at), the resulting phenotypic gap understates the genetic gap, which should be understood as the phenotypic difference in common environments.

We see an instance of this latter situation, I believe, in the next figure. Here, crime rates rather than IQ are on the vertical axis, and environments become less punitive and more conducive to crime as they move

---

[*] This is one aspect of "gene/environment correlation," which is discussed below.

[†] Here, as it does below, "common" means "common to" both races rather than "frequently encountered."

rightward. The positions of the curves are now switched, with B above W. While black crime rates have always exceeded white, it was only after 1960 that they reached their present high level. Since neither the black nor the white gene pools changed significantly between, say, 1920 and 1990, it might seem that the increase in black crime had to have been caused environmentally. Now, if a "cause" is a prior event sufficient for a given effect, the post-1960 jump in black crime must indeed have been caused by some event in the environment, [*] presumably the easing of sanctions against black (and white) offenders. In 1920, a black who killed a white, particularly in the South, faced almost certain death, whereas this was no longer the case by 1990. However, it does *not* follow that an environmental factor caused the race *difference* in crime rates in either era. The fact that easing of sanctions did not trigger an equal jump in *white* crime already indicates a race difference in responsiveness to changes in environment.

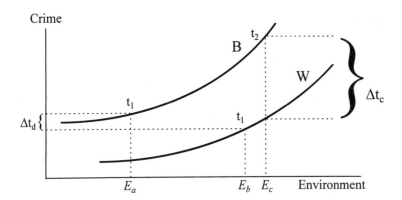

More significant, logically, than the absolute decrease in the severity of treatment of offenders was the convergence of treatment of blacks and whites; by 1990, the justice system held both races to the same, more lenient, rules. So imagine time t_1 to be 1920, t_2 to be 1990, E_a a "strict" environment, E_b a relaxed one, and E_c any common envi-

---

[*] This environmental change produced the jump in black crime only in conjunction with black genotypes. In the sense of a "cause" that denotes a necessary fixed background condition ("the car skidded because its tires were bald"), the black genotype is also a cause of increasing black crime.

ronment (in this case, a more "permissive" one). The race difference Δt_d in criminal behavior was small in 1920, when blacks and whites functioned in different criminal justice environments, but had widened to Δt_c by 1990 as the races came to function in the same environment. On this analysis, the present wide disparity in crime rates measures the genetic race difference in crime more accurately than did the narrow disparities of the past. An environment difference had cloaked a genetic difference.[*]

To put the main point most generally, it is a mistake to conclude that because environment can cause a change in a phenotype that it also causes differences *between* phenotypes. This mistake also vitiates much of the discussion of the Flynn effect (see Flynn 1984, 1987a, 1987b; Sowell 1995). Essentially, Flynn claims to have found that the IQs of all western populations have been rising at 3 points per decade since the 1930's, from which it follows that the mean IQ of contemporary whites is 15 points higher than that of whites in 1946, and therefore that contemporary blacks are on average as intelligent as whites of that time.[†] As with crime, the changes in black and white IQ have been too rapid to be genetic in origin. It is then argued that, since genes cannot explain the intergenerational 15-point rise in black and white IQs over the past 50 years, genes probably do not explain the 15-point difference between blacks and whites in any one generation.

Once again, the last step does not follow. Assuming the average IQs of both races have changed, the cause of these changes must indeed be environmental. However, the race *difference* has *not* changed. The most recent studies–Peoples, Fagan and Drotar (1995) and Brooks-Gunn, Klebanov and Duncan (1996)–find the full 15-point racial gap in IQ already established by age four. In terms of Figure 1, there may well be a Flynn factor pushing environments in a rightward, "favorable," direction, lifting both black and white phenotypes. However, in any *one* environment the IQ gap remains constant, suggesting a genetic difference in responsiveness to environmental change.

Environmentalists will reply that the constant IQ difference is a result of constant environmental inequalities concurrent with the Flynn

---

[*] This representation is inaccurate in some respects. In earlier times white authorities often turned a blind eye on black-on-black violence.

[†] This consequence of the Flynn effect is most puzzling. Is it plausible that the present American black population, left to itself, could build skyscrapers, develop an atom bomb or replicate other white achievements of the 1940s?

factor. This is a highly ad hoc interpretation, given that the overall black and white environments are converging, just as is the treatment of black and white criminals. Still, the very need to posit unknown environmental inequalities that balance the Flynn effect admits that the Flynn effect by itself is neutral about the cause of the race difference. A lockstep increase in black and white IQs over time shows at most that they respond identically to the Flynn factor, whatever that may be, not that they respond identically to all environmental factors.

A final interaction error is the assumption, made on both the Left and the Right, that all that matters morally about genetic race differences is whether such differences can be eliminated. Block and Jencks don't care whether there are genetic race differences because they can supposedly be eliminated by environmental manipulation. Herrnstein and Murray in *The Bell Curve* don't care whether there are genetic race differences because, they argue, an environmentally-caused IQ gap is as hard to reduce significantly as a genetic one. Both sides miss the point that the issues of white *guilt* and *responsibility* turn on why white IQs exceed that of blacks. Were procedures found tomorrow to lift black IQs to white levels, the currant race gap would still not be *wrong* if it resulted from genetic differences expressed in the environment in which both races have so far *actually functioned*. In that case whites would not be obligated to remedy the consequences of the gap by providing affirmative action or to close the gap itself by funding black IQ boosts.

An analogy makes this clear. Suppose Smith beats Jones in a race because genetic differences between them, interacting with the diets and training both received from birth, have expressed themselves in Smith's now being the faster runner. So long as Smith did not start before the gun, stop Jones from practicing, or otherwise wrong Jones, his victory was fair. That Jones could have outrun Smith had he received better training does not oblige Smith to surrender his trophy or see to it that Jones' children receive better training. The sheer possibility of Jones' running faster does not make anyone (except perhaps Jones' parents) remiss in not bringing that possibility about. So too, assuming the present race gap is not the result of white misdeeds, the discovery that black IQs can be raised would not show anything amiss with present black IQ levels, nor obligate whites (the only ones with the necessary resources) to administer IQ-boosts to blacks. Indeed, were it possible to change black genes directly so that blacks become more intelligent in the existing environment, whites would still have no obligation to finance the procedure.

Block's endorsement of an open-ended obligation to search–"we should...*simply try out new environments*"–merely shows that he has not thought the matter through. Goldberger and Manski more subtly exploit an ambiguity in the word "compensation." This usually means the nullification of some injury, but the injury to be nullified by "extreme compensation" as Manski and Goldberger understand it is the mean black genotype. This is an abuse of language, since the black genotype was not wrongly imposed by anyone, and is no more an injury than is the size of mice relative to cats an injury to mice. To talk of "compensating" a genetic limitation of blacks is to make whites responsible for a fact of nature.

The Question of Heritability

A concept related to interaction is that of heritability. Roughly speaking, the heritability of a phenotypic trait is the degree to which individual differences in that trait are due to individual genetic differences. As heritability fallacies play on the more technical aspects of heritability, however, a more precise definition is needed.

The total variation of a trait in a group, over the entire range of environments to which the group has been exposed, is the trait's *phenotypic variance* for that population. The total variation in the population's genes is the population's *genetic variance.*[*] The trait's heritability is then *the ratio of the genetic variance to the phenotypic variance.* Thus, in a population of genetically identical clones, the heritability of weight must be 0, since all variation in weight depends on variation in the environment. If in another population there is as much variation in the genes that influence weight as there is variation in weight, the heritability of weight reaches its other limiting value of 1.

Twin studies consistently demonstrate a high heritability for intelligence. Identical twins raised apart, differing only in their rearing environments, are far more alike in IQ (and many other traits) than random pairs of individuals and more alike even than fraternal twins raised in the same household. Environmentalists object that placement agencies may give separated twins to similar families and that reared-apart twins reunited by psychologists influence each other, but these factors cannot

---

[*] A trait's phenotypic variance is simply the square of the standard deviation of its distribution. Genotypic variance is trickier, since it too is defined in terms of population phenotypes. Full explanations for non-mathematical readers are given in Chapter 4 of Levin (1997).

begin to explain the extent of the similarity between twins. The best
current estimate of the heritability of IQ is 0.7, increasing to 0.8 toward
the end of the life-span as individuals increasingly shape their own environments.[*] The higher the heritability of a phenotype, the greater the
environmental disparity needed to explain a phenotypic gap of a given
size, hence the less likely the gap is to be caused solely by environment. I calculate in Levin (1997) that for an IQ of 15 points between
two individuals to be wholly environmental in origin, those individuals
must occupy environments more than two standard deviations apart, an
improbably large separation.

Given that a high heritability for IQ is beyond dispute, all an environmentalist can do is challenge the significance of heritability itself.
And many environmentalists duly contend that heritability is a scien-
tifically meaningless or "lousy" (Block 1995) concept.

The environmentalist challenge to heritability is based on the rela-
tivity of heritability to environments. We saw earlier that the heritability of a trait, for a given population, depends on how the trait varies.
Because of gene/environment interaction, however, a trait may show
much less variation in one set of environments than in another. For instance, weight in a population may vary between 140 and 270 lb. when
food is abundant, but vary between 120 and 150 lb. for a genetically
identical group when food is scarce. The heritability of weight is high
in the first case, where each individual's weight is determined by his
genetically determined metabolism, but low in the second, where the
scarcity of food cancels genetic differences in metabolization.

According to Lewontin, this shows that:

> the linear model [phenotypic variance = genetic variance + environ-
> mental variance] is a *local analysis*. It gives a result that depends
> upon the actual distribution of genotypes and environments in the
> particular population sampled. Therefore, the result of the analysis
> has a historical (i.e., spatiotemporal) limitation and is not in general
> a statement about *functional* relations . . . [T]he particular distribu-
> tion of genotypes and environments in a given population at a given
> time picks out relations from the array of reaction norms that are
> necessarily atypical of the entire spectrum of causative relations. .
> .The analysis of causes in human genetics is meant to provide us
> with the basic knowledge we require for correct schemes of envi-
> ronmental modification and intervention. . . . Analysis of variance
> can do neither of these because its results are a unique function of

---

[*] This is another example of gene/environment correlation.

the present distribution of environment and genotypes (1976c:183-192).

Lewontin moves much too quickly. The ratio of genotypic to phenotypic variance in a limited group of environments is a perfectly well-defined statistic. It does not tell us everything we want to know about a genotype, but it tells us something. Without infallibly predicting the behavior of a genotype everywhere, heritability over a varied range of environments permits informed guesses about phenotypes in unexamined ones. When a trait such as intelligence has appeared in the same form in every ecological niche yet colonized by humans, it may reasonably be expected to emerge in like form in new niches. Ensembles of environments do not become "necessarily atypical" simply by falling short of exhaustiveness.[*]

Lewontin's criticism of heritability is simply the old philosophical problem of induction applied to genetic variation. That something has always happened a certain way is no *guarantee* that it will continue to. It does not follow from the fact that copper has always conducted electricity on Earth that it conducts electricity in other galaxies, or that it will conduct electricity on Earth tomorrow. Likewise, intelligence is relatively fixed in known environments but might conceivably vary wildly in so-far unknown ones. These points of logic, however, have nothing to do with what is *likely* to happen. No one has yet figured out how to prove that the future will resemble the past, but scientists have no hesitation in extrapolating from the known to the unknown absent specific reasons not to. Without some specific reason to believe in environments over the horizon with which intelligence genes interact in novel ways, the present heritability of intelligence is a good guide to the overall importance of genes.

A less extreme environmentalist argument runs that high between-individual heritability, the sort of heritability discussed so far, is irrelevant to heritability between groups. Average body weight in an environment with adequate food might be, say, 180 lb. while the average weight of a genetically identical population in an impoverished environment might be 135 lb. Although weight is substantially heritable in both groups, the difference in average weight is due entirely to the difference in food availability. According to a similar argument, individual heritability of IQ might be high for both whites and blacks, but the average black and white IQs differ solely because white children experience more stimulating environments.

---

[*] Similar points are made in Sesardic (1993).

I believe hereditarians have too readily conceded the within-group/between-group distinction–not that this concession destroys hereditarianism. Jensen points out that while the two kinds of heritability may be *logically* distinct, high individual heritability for a trait is *evidence* that genes contribute to group variation. Rushton shrewdly notes environmentalist special pleading in the assumption that, since environmental factors explain some individual variation in IQ, they must explain group variation as well. But there is a more forceful reply. The logic of estimating the role of genes in group differences is *precisely the same* as that of estimating the role of genes in individual differences.

To ask whether environment alone can explain a phenotypic difference in IQ between two given individuals is in effect to ask how likely the given gap would be if those individuals were identical twins. The higher the (individual) heritability of IQ, as explained earlier, the more widely separated their environments would have to be, and the wider that separation, the less likely it is. *An identical analysis applies to mean group phenotypic differences.* For environment alone to explain the race difference, the average genotypes of the two races must be identical. To say that the average black/white gap is totally environmental in origin is, in other words, to say that the average white and the average black are identical twins. Assuming the individual heritability of IQ to be the same for blacks and whites, calculations like those done for individuals indicate how far apart the races' mean environments must be, and how common such widely spaced pairs of environments are. The higher the *individual* heritability of IQ is, the less likely it becomes that the mean black/white difference is purely environmental.

Proceeding as in the individual case, an environmental cause for the 15-point racial IQ gap requires a gap of more than two standard deviations between typical black and white environments, a gap not often encountered. Of course, the issue cannot be resolved by statistical means alone. The actual dissimilarity of black and white environments is a factual question (pursued in Levin 1997 following Jensen 1973), as is the actual dissimilarity of the environments of any two individuals. The points on which I am insisting are that within- and between-group heritabilities are structurally similar, and that the probability of a genetic contribution to a group difference rises as the individual heritability of IQ does.

A last effort to undermine the significance of heritability focuses on *gene/environment correlation.* The basic idea, again accepted by all sides, is that genes influence not only the bodies and minds of their home organisms but the kinds of environment these organisms occupy. A man genetically disposed to exercise may choose an environment enabling him to, perhaps by building a tennis court or living in an environment suitable for jogging. As a consequence, the "exercise gene" is not sprinkled randomly across environments, but occurs disproportionately often in those that favor exercise. You will find lots of exercise genes in the vicinity of tennis courts. This gene/environment relation is not necessarily inter*active*, since the genes correlated with an environment need not be the ones shaping it. Genetically high-IQ children usually have books handy, not because the children purchase books, but because their high-IQ parents, who bequeath their offspring good genes, also buy books for them. Giftedness genes correlate with reading matter without causing the correlation.

Enter the environmentalist, objecting that gene/environment correlation leads heritability estimates to include environmental effects. Take exercise once again. How often someone exercises depends on unarguably biological factors like vigor, but also on environment: residents of Southern California can and will get more outdoor exercise than genetically identical habitants of the Arctic. However, since an athletic genotype tends to chose environments conducive to exercise, it will be associated with exercise not simply by coding for biological vigor, but by encouraging a person to locate where exercise is available. Heritability conflates both sources of the gene/exercise association, counting as genetic such environmental effects as the availability of tennis courts.

As so far stated this is a non-problem, for the effects on an organism of an environment produced by the organism's genes certainly *should* count as genetic. Phenotypes need not end at the skin. A tennis court built by a man to indulge his genetically-determined desire to exercise expresses his genes as surely as does his height, and the level of fitness he reaches by using that court daily is as much an effect of his genes as is his genetically determined metabolism.

Block (1995) and Jencks (1992) reply, in effect, that gene-induced environmental factors can affect organisms in quite another way. Suppose–Block's example–hair color is genetically determined, but non-redheads regularly bang redheads over the head with baseball bats. Genes for red hair will be closely associated with low IQ, and the heritability of IQ correspondingly high, because red hair provokes an IQ-lowering societal reaction, yet it would be perverse (argues Block) to term such group differences in IQ genetic. If genetic race is associated with low IQ because black skin color diminishes the expectations of teachers, which then diminishes the intellectual performance of black children, the race difference in IQ should also be considered socially caused.

How great a problem possibilities like Block's present for heritability estimates depends on their frequency. They are certainly not prominent in the genetic literature, where most gene/environment correlations studied are of the athletes-building-tennis-courts or parents-stimulating-offspring sort. The increase in heritability of IQ with age, as individuals increasingly control the stimuli they receive, is a typical finding. Such reactive correlations as are discussed tend to be those in which phenotypes are *amplified* rather than diminished, as when a curious child stirs adult responses that stimulate his curiosity.

With regard to race, Block's analogy is off-base. To see why, suppose the average redhead in Block's hypothetical world were found to perform most poorly on the tests of mental ability that were most heritable. The beatings administered to redheads could not explain this correlation, since they would presumably depress redhead mental abilities uniformly. We would conclude, faced with such data, that the redhead/brunette IQ gap probably *was* genetic in origin after all, the cudgeling notwithstanding. To conclude otherwise would require, in effect, that brunettes hit redheads harder on those parts of the noggin protecting brain functions under genetic control—too great a concidence to be believed.

Now, concerning race, it appears that the black/white gap on mental tests does in fact increase with test heritability. To conclude that the gap is nonetheless due to racist reactions to skin color is to believe that whites somehow calibrate their abuse of blacks to inhibit most strongly those aspects of mental functioning most under genetic control. Such pre-established disharmony is not impossible, but it is most unlikely.

In any case, the redhead analogy is inappropriate because whites do not egregiously mistreat blacks. American blacks are now, in some respects, a privileged class, enjoying preference in employment, schooling, the right to disrupt the free association of whites, and solicitude when victimized by white offenders. A white who did attack a black with a baseball bat would not only be guilty of assault but face federal civil rights charges as well. Indeed, about 80 percent of interracial violent crime consists of blacks assaulting whites. As for the treatment of blacks in the past, school segregation—exhibit A in the case against whites—was hardly an "assault," since the schools blacks were permitted to attend were far superior to any educational institution ever created by a black society. It can thus be argued that Jim Crow was a *stimulating* environment and that the integrated schools blacks now attend are even more stimulating.

But Block's error is not simply empirical. To see why, let's "deconstruct" his "discourse." Why does he draw an analogy involving *hair*?[*] No doubt because hair is a literally superficial, indeed physically detachable trait. Once race is viewed as equally external, societal reactions to skin color appear entirely irrational, and not only should not count as genetic but deserve no respect at all. As the depth of race differences becomes increasingly apparent, this sort of analogy will seem increasingly silly.

I will be brief in treating the final error about inheritance that has percolated through the environmentalist literature, for the topic is somewhat technical. I have in mind the claim that blacks and whites separated too recently in evolutionary time for an IQ gap to have evolved.

Assessment of this claim depends on how wide the race gap is, how long the races have been apart, and two associated variables called "intensity of selection" and "selection against recessives." The question is whether it is possible to find in nature the values these variables would have had to attain in order for the known race difference to have evolved in the time during which the races are known to have been apart. The answer, worked out in detail in Levin (1997), is "Yes, easily."

The best estimate of the current mean IQ of black Africans is 73, 27 points below the white mean. The best estimate of the time of the black/white split, when pioneers from Africa entered the Eurasian land mass, is a bit over 100,000 years ago. The mean IQ of both the African and offshoot populations may be assumed to have been 73 at the start of the process. IQ rose to 100 in Eurasia, presumably as the harsher conditions in Eurasia selected against low intelligence more intensely than did conditions in Africa. Using standard methods of quantitative genetics it can be shown that the intensity of selection necessary to achieve a 27-point change in 4,000 generations (1 generation = 25 years) is 0.00082, which means, roughly speaking, that each generation in Europe had to be about 1/80 of an IQ point smarter than its predecessor. That this rate of change in turn is genetically possible can be shown by means of a simple additive model in which phenotypic intelligence depends on two alleles at 100 gene loci. In that model, an in-

---

[*] Jencks 1992 also argues a point identical to Block's in terms of a hair analogy.

tensity of selection of 0.00082 corresponds to a rate of selection against "recessives" of 0.000106. Operationally, this requires that, in the Eurasian subgroup, just 11 fewer individuals per 100,000 with a "recessive" allele" at one locus reproduced as compared to the African stay-at-homes. As natural processes go, a rate of selection against recessives of 0.000106 is *extremely small*. In the wild and in laboratory experiments genotypes have been observed to change as much as 1,000 times faster. Dramatic shifts in the coloration of moths and the learning behavior of mice have been achieved in 40 generations, with rates of selection as high as 0.2 or 0.3. There has been plenty of time for race differences to evolve.

The Environmentalist Style

A few general remarks about the style of environmentalist writing remain to be made.

Earlier I remarked on the nonstandard and needlessly complex mathematical notation in the passage from Goldberger and Manski (1995). (They also offer a "translation" of Herrnstein and Murray into the language of econometrics whose only apparent purpose is to intimidate nonmathematical readers.) I would also add Lewontin's (1976c) explanation of "the linear model of heritability" in the passage cited above in the section on heritability, which includes a display of the equation $Y - \mu_Y = (G - \mu_Y) + (E - \mu_Y) + (GE) = e$, written, he admits, "in a slightly different way than it is usually displayed" (182). In the same context he explains his criticism of heritability, paraphrased on p. 80 above, as the "need for functions of the form $(E - \mu_Y) = f(T - \mu_T)$ and $GE = h[(g - \mu_g), (T - \mu_T)]$." These are the only mathematical expressions Lewontin uses, but they come at a point that makes most of his article inaccessible to non-mathematical readers. These abuses of technicality recall the mathematician Leonhard Euler's debate with the atheist (and mathematical tyro) Denis Diderot before the Russian court. Euler announced a proof of God's existence, wrote $e^{i\pi} + 1 = 0$ on a blackboard, and challenged Diderot to reply. The bluff worked: Diderot fled in confusion.

In my experience, the most clearly stated arguments are usually the most cogent ones. Writers fall back on technical jargon when they themselves do not trust their own views to be persuasive when stated clearly. Let the reader beware of environmentalist bluffs.

The reader may wonder why I have neglected that most common environmentalist fallacy, the allegation that hereditarian thinking is dangerous. I am so impatient with this outrageous tactic that I dislike even considering it. I don't like to see the debate mired in "free speech" issues when the really important subject is race itself. So let the last word be not mine but David Hume's: "When any opinion leads to absurdity, it is certainly false; but it is not certain that an opinion is false because it is of dangerous consequence. Such topics, therefore, ought entirely to be forborne as serving nothing to the discovery of truth, but only to make the person of an antagonist odious."

References

Part of this talk was based on material in Levin (1997). To avoiding distracting references and footnotes, I have omitted some documentation supplied in that work.

Baumrind, D. 1991. "To Nurture Nature." *Behavioral and Brain Sciences* 14: 386-387.

Block, N. 1995. "How Heritability Misleads about Race." *Cognition* 56: 99-128.

Block, N., and Dworkin, G. 1976. "IQ, Heritability and Inequality." In Block and Dworkin, eds., *The IQ Controversy.* New York: Pantheon: 410-540.

Brooks-Gunn, J., Klebanov, P., and Duncan, G. 1996. "Ethnic Differences in Children's Intelligence Test Scores: Role of Economic Deprivation, Home Environment and Maternal Characteristics," *Child Development* 67: 396-408.

Caccone, A., and Powell, J. 1989. "DNA Divergence Among Hominoids." *Evolution* 43: 925-942.

Cavalli-Sforza, L., Menozzi, P., and Piazza, A. 1993. "Demic Expansions and Human Evolution." *Science* 259: 639-646.

_____. 1984. "The Mean IQ of Americans: Massive Gains 1932 to 1978." *Psychological Bulletin* 95: 29-51.

_____. 1987a. "Massive IQ Gains in 14 Nations: What IQ Tests Really Measure." *Psychological Bulletin* 101: 171-191.

_____. 1987b. "Race and IQ: Jensen's Case Refuted." In Modgil and Modgil, eds.: 221-232.

Goldberger, A., and Manski, C. 1995. "Review Article: *The Bell Curve* by Herrnstein and Murray." *Journal of Economic Literature* 33: 762-776.

Gould, S. 1995. "Age-Old Fallacies of Thinking and Stinking." *Natural History*, June: 6-13.

Jencks, C. 1992. *Rethinking Social Policy*. Cambridge, Mass.: Harvard University Press.

Jensen, A. 1973. *Educability and Group Differences*. New York: Harper and Row.

Layzer, D. 1976. "Science of Superstition? A Physical Scientist Looks at the IQ Controversy." In Block and Dworkin, eds.: 194-241.

Levin, M. 1997. *Why Race Matters*. Westport, CT: Praeger.

Lewontin, R. 1976a. "Race and Intelligence." In Block and Dworkin, eds.: 78-92.

_____. 1976b. "Further Remarks on Race and Intelligence." In Block and Dworkin, eds.: 107-112.

_____. 1976c. "The Analysis of Variance and the Analysis of Cause." In Block and Dworkin, eds.: 179-193.

Peoples, C., Fagan, J., and Drotar, D. 1995. "The Influence of Race on 3-year-old Children's Performance on the Stanford-Binet: Fourth Edition," *Intelligence* 21: 69-82.

Sowell, T. 1995. "Ethnicity and IQ." *The American Spectator*, February: 32-36.

ଓଃ

CRsO

Towards Renewal and Renaissance

Fr. James Thornton

I am greatly honored to have been invited to address this assembly of men and women who seek some deliverance from the contemporary dilemma surrounding the question of race. This question has bedeviled our poor country for the better part of two centuries, and has brought about in our history expenditures in human lives and treasure of tragic proportions. Of late, it threatens thoroughly to overwhelm us and transform this nation, totally and permanently, into a national and social entity radically dissimilar to that represented by the past four hundred years of our history.

We have come to think it curious that a committed Christian would have an opinion on the subject of race not consonant with the prevailing and rather rigorously invoked view and would express that personal opinion in a public forum. For in these closing years of the twentieth century, Christianity has come to be looked upon by some as a religion for the fainthearted and the perfidious, as a kind of fifth column within our European culture, and as one of the seeds of European man's own destruction. However, I do not agree with that view, needless to say.

Yet, I would be the first to admit that among those who call themselves "Christians," and especially within the leadership councils of certain official, mainstream, ostensibly Christian groups, there are multitudes of spiritual charlatans and cultural Bolsheviks who, as one perceptive writer put it many years ago, nourish their diseased souls "with dreams of blood and burning cities." However, I would insist that these men do not represent genuine, historical Christianity as it has been understood through the centuries. Just as the early Church was disturbed by heretical offshoots that amalgamated elements of Christianity with some of the more bizarre forms of paganism, so in our day do we witness the proliferation of heretical, sectarian modes of thought. These are perfectly described by the Russian Orthodox philosopher and sociologist Pitirim Sorokin in these words:

a wild concoction of a dozen various 'Social Gospels,' diversified
by several beliefs of Christianity diluted by those of Marxism, Democracy, and Theosophy, enriched by a dozen vulgarized philosophical ideas, corrected by several scientific theories, peacefully
squatting side by side with the most atrocious magical superstitions.

What he refers to, of course, is the World Council of Churches kind
of Christianity–that artificial, ideological, politically correct substitute
for the original product. It is, indeed, the very antithesis of traditional
Christianity.

I contend that our magnificent European culture, stretching across
the North American continent eastward through Europe to the Urals
(and incorporating some outlying areas such as Australia and New
Zealand), is one of the matchless and wonderful gifts of Christianity, of
Christian teaching, of Christian civilization. We need only think for a
moment of buildings such as Notre Dame, Chartres, Justinian's Hagia
Sophia, San Marco in Venice, San Vitale and Sant' Apollinare in
Ravenna, and Dormition and Annunciation Cathedrals in Moscow;
works of architecture of matchless beauty; buildings, all of them, that
still, even in this age of skyscrapers, produce gasps of awe from those
blessed to visit them.

We need only think, too, of the literature of the Christian European
peoples–Dante, Shakespeare, Milton, Cervantes, Schiller, Goethe,
Dostoyevsky–of the music–Bach, Handel, Mozart, Beethoven, Berlioz,
Bruckner, Rachmaninoff–and of the great works of art–Fra Angelico,
Titian, Raphael, Michelangelo, Dürer, Rembrandt, Rublev. I mention
only a few names from each field; to list all those of importance, the
whole role of honor, so to speak, would take hours and hours. But the
point is that virtually all of the works of creative genius of the past
2,000 years, all that we admire as monuments of high culture, all of
those things that nurture the spirits of refined men and women, come
from Christian civilization, that wonderful fusion of the creative genius
of the European peoples with the refining, elevating genius of Christianity.

Pre-Christian, ancient Mediterranean civilization, with its own great
accomplishments in philosophy, law, sculpture, architecture, and so
forth, had by the second century of the Christian Era reached an im-
passe. The tremendous edifice erected by the ancients was rapidly
crumbling by then, and was in danger of being lost forever. But this did
not happen. Christianity took dying Græco-Roman civilization, perfected and transformed it to a remarkable degree, and imparted new life
to it. In the West this was done under the auspices of barbarian tribes

who very slowly absorbed aspects of the dying pagan civilization they found, and who, though they possessed no real understanding of this civilization for a long time, after some centuries of comparative darkness, gave birth to Western European civilization.

In the East the process was different. The Empire, and Græco-Roman civilization, lived on under New Rome, under Constantinople. What took place there was, in the words of the renowned scholar Father Georges Florovsky, "a conversion of the Hellenic mind and heart" or, to put it another way, the "Christianization of Hellenism." And the achievements of the resulting Eastern European Christian civilization–first in Byzantium and then in Old Russia–are incomparable. So Christianity, far from the "culture destroyer" or "culture distorter" of Nietzsche, et al., was a premier culture preserver and profound culture creator. Both in the Eastern and Western halves of Europe, civilization and culture sprang forth from Christianity; they are Christian.

What interests us here today is the culture sickness that seems to have infected European mankind over the whole of the globe, a sickness that seems slowly to be pulling us downward towards some unknown fate, towards some terrible void. I suggest that we have come to this melancholy state today precisely because the old traditions of European Christian civilization have been lost. Were Christianity as vital today as, say, 1,000 years ago, or 500 years ago, or even 150 years ago, the state of affairs in which we now find ourselves would be impossible. What brought us to this unhappy condition? Why is the way of life of our American and European forebears dissolving around us?

Many men have analyzed this question; to name only a few, Juan Donoso-Cortés, Friedrich Nietzsche, Konstantine Pobiedonostev, Jacob Burckhardt, Oswald Spengler, José Ortega y Gasset, and the twentieth-century American Richard Weaver. All grasped that our way of life was at grave risk, that those concepts and ideals which we value so highly were in danger, and that a profound sickness had descended on our civilization. Insofar as precise diagnosis is concerned, many would disagree with the others. Some were Christians and some were not. Nietzsche contended that Christianity had exhausted itself and that a new system of morality should replace it, for the sake of the survival of civilization. Spengler, as I am sure you know, believed that the fate of European man was inevitable, that he had lived out his natural, allotted span of time and now must face his doom. Others, like Sorokin, held out the hope that civilization might regenerate itself through a spiritual awakening and live on for many hundreds of years to come. I will not argue the precise merits of each of these points of view, though I will now briefly discuss the thoughts of two of them.

In re-reading one of the most interesting works of the nineteenth-century Swiss historian, Jacob Burckhardt, his posthumously published *Reflections on History*, I was struck by his extraordinary insights into the pathologies that were then beginning to attack European civilization. Those pathologies are no different today, though they have advanced to a critical stage. I readily admit that my interpretation of Burckhardt is not the usual one. Burckhardt was an elliptical thinker whose ideas are open to more than one interpretation and whose writings contain many valuable messages. Those familiar with *Reflections on History* know that Burckhardt speaks of the interaction within societies between three primary institutions: Church, State, and Culture. The terms Church and State require no definition here, the meanings of the words are obvious. However, Burckhardt's use of the word Culture requires some elucidation.

Culture, in Burckhardt's scheme, is very broad and encompasses just about everything not included in the first two. In Burckhardt's words, "[Culture's] total external form. . . , as distinguished from the State and religion, is society in its broadest sense" or, as he also puts it, "Culture may be defined as the sum total of those mental developments which take place spontaneously and lay no claim to universal or compulsory authority." History after the rise of Christianity is the record of a long rivalry between Church and State. Both tend, however, to be very conservative forces and, though they compete for power, both inhibit Culture, which tends to be revolutionary. The most revolutionary of the forces within Culture is money-making, that is, the economy.

From the time of Constantine until the French Revolution, Church and State acted successfully to keep Culture circumscribed, particularly its money-making component. Since the time of the French Revolution, the prestige of both Church and State have suffered and Culture has broken loose, so to speak. The State has now become the instrument of Culture, and to some extent the Church too. Economic Man, in both his capitalistic and Marxian incarnations, sits triumphant, bestriding the whole globe.

Let us note that Burckhardt is not categorical about these things, but merely suggests. He writes, "We need not wish ourselves back into the Middle Ages, but we should try to understand them. Our life is a business, theirs was living. The people as a totality hardly existed, but that which was of the people flourished. Thus what we are wont to regard as moral progress is the domestication of individuality brought about (a) by the versatility and wealth of culture and (b) by the vast increase in the power of the State over the individual, which may even lead to the complete abdication of the individual, more especially where money-making predominates to the exclusion of everything else, ultimately absorbing all initiative."

A few lines later, he adds, "The arrogant belief in the moral superiority of the present . . . has only fully developed of late years; it makes no exceptions, even in favor of classical antiquity. The secret mental reservation is that money-making is today easier and safer than ever. Were that menaced, the exaltation it engenders would collapse." And, ponder these prophetic words from Burckhardt: "Money-making, the main force of present-day culture, postulates the universal State, if only for the sake of communications . . . ." To Burckhardt, unrestrained money-making, the obsession with materialism, the "bourgeoisification" of the spirit of European man, are dangerous things.

I believe that Burckhardt touches on the heart of the problem of European man. So long as Church, State, and Culture interacted with one another in an organic fashion, curbing one another and thereby holding back certain darker human proclivities, then our European civilization remained essentially healthy. Once these institutions were uncoupled from one another, thanks to the forces loosed by the Enlightenment, the foundations of the structure of our civilization began to disintegrate.

Contemplate, for a moment, the reality of contemporary television, radio, films, entertainment, music, advertising, painting, sculpture, and so on–all powerful elements of a culture without restraints. Consider how our present culture sickness undermines the authority of the traditions of society, of family, of morality, of religion, of nation, of language. Rightly is it said that the great crisis of our age is a crisis of the breakdown of authority. Our modern commercial, hedonistic society denies the father authority over his family, the parent authority over his child, the law authority over miscreants, the priest authority over his flock, the Church authority over sinners, man authority over the living things of the Earth, and God authority over His creation.

More than likely, such propensities are intrinsic characteristics of the commercial way of thinking that makes money the king of all and the final arbiter of right and wrong, that atomizes the community, that transforms citizens into consumers and units of production. They are innate in an economic-rationalist mode of thought that teaches that materialistic self-interest is the engine of human history and human society, that holds that men do live by bread alone. Other diagnosti-

cians of the disorders of our age have written similarly. Burckhardt is
not alone in his diagnosis. Hilaire Belloc, G. K. Chesterton, and R. H.
Tawney (curiously, Tawney was a man of the Left), and the economist
Wilhelm Roepke have expressed similar concerns.

If money is king and money-making the ultimate criterion, if materialistic self-interest is the engine of history, if men do live by bread
alone, then what utility is there in the preservation of the unique civilization of European man? Does not some sort of "global village" with a
world culture make far more economic sense? The more uniform the
habits, tastes, and mores of the peoples of the world, the easier to do
business, the easier for some to make money. It is expressive of our
current predicament that such discourse as is now allowed in the matter
of Third-World immigration to North America revolves exclusively
around economic arguments, the economic advantages or disadvan-
tages of immigration, one side demonstrating that more and more consumers automatically equal more and more prosperity and the other
side arguing to the contrary. A young American, supposedly a conservative, recently told me that he does not believe that Third-World immigration is a problem and that if we can simply stimulate the economy
to grow more quickly, such growth will solve all concerns about immigration. Would that the things of this world were that easy!

Richard Weaver's critique of modernity is similar in some respects
to the foregoing. He discusses "the creation of a class of 'functionalists'
called 'businessmen'," and he quotes approvingly a passage from a
work by Professor Elijah Jordan which reads as follows:

> In business intelligent and serious interpretation of facts is never
> called for; intelligence is not involved at all. Only the individual
> with the strongest motives, motives least checked by moral sensi-
> tiveness, can survive. The psychological make-up of the business
> 'mind' is therefore a mere collection of disconnected motives, im-
> pulses entirely without conscious direction or moral unity of pur-
> pose, hence without intelligence.

Without conscious direction; without moral unity of purpose; without intelligence. And yet terms such as "the American Way of Life"
and "the American Dream" are almost exclusively associated with this
successful business mentality; they are formulated in materialistic, even
hedonistic, terms. That type of thinking dominates our nation, and
much of today's world. Ask even most modern "conservatives" in
America and Europe what they stand for, and the glories of our economic system and our prosperity will form the desiccated heart and
soul of their ideological analysis–the so-called conservative philosophy

will be shot through with materialism, although there is nothing conservative in the commercial *Weltanschauung*. By its very nature, the unfettered money-making mentality tends always to wreak havoc on traditional relationships within society, the traditional hierarchy and patriarchy of European custom, the traditional family, traditional religion and morality, and the traditional ways of life.

• Is it any wonder that since successful money-making has become the ultimate criterion for our society, that education has become a kind of glorified job training and that to make education into job training, traditional curricula–from classical languages and history to philosophy and great literature–have been largely abandoned? One can become prosperous with an MBA, but probably not with an MA in classical Greek or Ancient History.

• Is it any wonder that entertainment, literature, films, and the like have become the domain of degenerates whose products flow straight to our youth from moral and intellectual cesspits? There are vast sums of dollars to be made from such cultural sewage, and men become rich thereby. Since becoming rich is considered the supremely admirable quality these days, such men are admired above all others.

• Is it any wonder that rock "music" has supplanted nearly all other musical forms? Rock "music" and its multiform appurtenances, are the very quintessence of decadence. Rock music celebrates primitiveness, is soddened in nihilism, and luxuriates in barren, loveless sexuality. It is a musical lowest common denominator and so possesses colossal appeal today. With absolutely no musical aptitude or knowledge, people nevertheless make millions and tens of millions of dollars. Thus, such music generates huge revenues, so much so that it is one of America's great export products. More importantly, perhaps, it represents the negation of genuine musical culture, which draws its inspiration from particular national cultures, and represents its replacement with the artificial, rootless, pseudo-culture of internationalism. It is the perfect music for the new world order, the perfect accompaniment for life in a "global village."

• Is it any wonder that illegal drugs are a source of spreading chaos and tremendous pain in contemporary American and European societies? I believe that it may be declared with confidence that our current money-oriented society will never take decisive action against the drug barons at home and abroad who have done so much to corrupt our society in the past thirty-five years. The corruption already touches the upper echelons of both major political parties, and so apart from certain gestures and political posturing about the issue, nothing will be done.

• Finally, is it any wonder that enjoyment of the "good life" by most ordinary citizens necessitates such drastic limitations on family size that in virtually every nation of the European world, birthrates have fallen considerably below replacement level? Thanks to money-mindedness and hedonism, we are a dying breed.

If obsession with money, that is the commercial worldview, has brought us near collapse, it can come as no surprise that, with regard to questions surrounding America's racial dilemma, short-term economic considerations supersede all other considerations. When one contemplates the kind of well-ordered society we had fifty, or sixty, or eighty years ago, the conclusion is inescapable that for primarily the economic enrichment of certain groups and individuals, the country is being systematically strip-mined, culturally speaking.

Rightly did Solzhenitsyn speak of our heritage being trampled upon by the party mob in the East and the commercial mob in the West. This is sensed by many ordinary citizens who for good reason feel threatened by the societal revolution that has overtaken us in the past forty years. Whatever hope we have seems to reside with ordinary Americans, especially those of the lower middle-class who no longer enjoy so great a measure of material prosperity as heretofore. Though they are confused by a continual spate of propaganda from the organs of the mass media, nevertheless they know in their hearts–at the deeper levels of their consciousness–the source of their gathering troubles. To bring these people to a realization of their priceless Christian European heritage, and its source, is therefore essential for the resurrection of this country and of the West.

I wish here briefly to mention another diagnostician of our current time of troubles, the sociologist Pitirim Sorokin. Sixty years ago, Sorokin wrote that healthy cultures are integrated unities. Art, architecture, music, literature, philosophy, ethics, morals, government, and religion are all interrelated with one another. Useful elements may be drawn from foreign cultures, so long as they do not contradict the unity of the host culture, and so long as they are modified and digested, so as to become wholly a part of that unity.

Until relatively recently, our own European culture was just such a unity, consistent throughout the multiplicity of its numberless aspects and elements. Drawing that which is valuable from other cultures (for instance, Hindu-Arabic numerals), it digested these things, so that they became completely part of its unity. The values of this healthy culture were still strong, its creativity still vigorous, its "soul" still undefiled. That which was intrinsically contradictory it rejected, since, as a healthy entity, it was highly selective and discriminatory. Now, however, the picture has changed. Our society is no longer healthy, but is sick or perhaps dying. While still robust, still believing in itself, its genius created a grand civilization. This creativity, however, has now been lost. It can no longer discriminate between the useful and dangerous, and, consequently, everything pours in and takes root in our unhealthy culture, often to the exclusion of the healthy, formerly unified elements.

As the flood of undigested, foreign elements becomes greater and greater, the host culture becomes more distorted, more sickly, and less able to protect itself. Thus, the host culture undergoes disintegration, at times more slowly and at other times more rapidly. We may observe all of this in our contemporary culture which, in its variety of undigested elements, is utterly astonishing. Literally everything and anything can be found within it, each loudly competing for our attention and allegiance. All possess "rights" equal to those of every other, and all enjoy equal tolerance by society. Between that which is venerable and native, and that which is new and foreign, there are absolutely no distinctions. So it is with a society that has lost faith in the source of its greatness; so it is when a living ideal no longer exists to inspire it. Sorokin insisted that this loss of faith was rooted in excessive materialism and that a return to a more spiritual manner of thinking and acting was the only hope for saving civilization.

Interestingly, Richard Weaver writes similarly in his book, *Visions of Order*. He observes that the spirit of a culture "always operates positively by transfiguring and excluding. It is of the essence of culture to feel its own imperative and to believe in the uniqueness of its worth. . . . Syncretistic cultures, like syncretistic religions, have always proved relatively powerless to create and influence. . . . Culture derives its very desire to continue from its unitariness."

I have given you some thoughts, borrowed from some great thinkers of the nineteenth and twentieth centuries, touching on one or two aspects of our crisis. My poor utterances are not meant to be the ultimate word on this question, far from it. Rather I have striven to show that the racial dilemma does not exist in isolation, but is part of a whole matrix in which we are bound, which is itself the consequence of evil choices made by our forebears long ago.

I wish now to say a few words at this point specifically on the question of race. One of the most valuable sociological attributes of traditional Christianity since its founding two thousand years ago has been its recognition that human beings are not equal. Christianity, it is quite true, holds that all men are equal when standing before the throne of God at the Last Judgement. But, apart from that, the doctrine that human beings are, or should be, equal in a worldly sense appears nowhere in Christian teaching. That human beings are intellectually equal, or that such differences as do exist in individuals or groups are rooted, for example, in economic deprivation, would have been preposterous notions to most traditional Christian thinkers and teachers of past ages. That all cultures or peoples of the world are equally suitable as bearers of high Christian civilization would have been a laughable proposition to these men.

No, traditional Christianity believes that healthy societies are socially diverse and that a healthy society is organized hierarchically, with different orders and classes and with the differing material conditions and privileges appropriate to those orders and classes, as Russell Kirk once wrote. We see this in the very organization of the Church itself, with its many distinct levels: clergy and laity; Archbishops, Bishops, Archpriests, Priests, Deacons, Subdeacons, and so forth. The levels of responsibility attained correspond to the special God-given gifts of each, in accordance with the needs of the Church. Certainly, that elaborate, consciously hierarchical organization, entwined by the symbols of sacred mystery and blessed by the Church, is evident in every Christian society, from that of Constantine and Justinian all the way down through the centuries to that of Nicholas II. It was true in Western Europe as well as Eastern Europe.

I must add here parenthetically that to those moderns who are inclined to denigrate Byzantine civilization, or Western Medieval civilization, let it be remembered that these civilizations were extremely successful, maintaining a high degree of order and giving birth to high cultures of unparalleled achievement and quality, and remaining culturally productive for many centuries—in the case of Byzantium for almost a thousand years.

The Fathers of the Church taught that just as the spiritual world is organized hierarchically, so too should be the earthly world; any other kind of societal structure was regarded as something demonic, in that it promotes spiritual and societal disorder. The Fathers believed that God abhors chaos, that in a Christian society the earthly order should properly reflect the heavenly order, and that egalitarianism and rule by the mob, that is rule according to the whims and lusts of the herd, are injurious to the morals of Christians and to the fabric of the Christian community. Clearly, if the Christian ideal is that human society is constituted in aristocratic, hierarchical fashion, and if this kind of constitution is regarded as something of divine origin, so it is implicit in such theories of organization that men are not created equal insofar as their innate abilities are concerned. Christianity is clearly not a religion of earthly egalitarianism.

Our own country is rooted in a somewhat different philosophical tradition, but even here no objective scholar would dispute that the Founders of this nation, most of whom were Christians, did not believe in the inherent equality of individual men or of races, apart from the idea that free men should be equal in the eyes of the law. In no other sense were men born equal. Certain it is that insofar as this country was traditional in its religious beliefs, it strongly believed in the superiority of its European-derived way of life. There could be no question of overthrowing that order. Insofar as deeply felt religious belief waned, and a materialistic ideology replaced that religious belief, feelings of inferiority, of false guilt, and of confusion have tended to prevail.

John Baker, in his volume *Race*, published by Oxford University Press in the 1970s, suggests that a marked sense of racial differences has existed in mankind for thousands of years, certainly during all of recorded history, and very likely in pre-historic times. Italian sociologist Corrado Gini writes similarly, showing how all ethnic or racial groups exhibit a strong consciousness of human ethnic differences with a preference for their own. Now, some, most notably Marxists and liberals, may decry this inclination which seems to be intrinsic to human nature, yet it is nonetheless an indisputable fact of man's existence. Towards the Canaanites, the ancient Hebrews showed, as Baker puts it, a "marked disrespect." Virtually all outsiders, according to the reckoning of the ancient Greeks, were barbarians. Even among certain primitive tribes of Africa, there is evidently a belief that some of the even more primitive tribes are inferior. How has Christianity dealt with these facts? Until fairly recently, especially the last fifty or sixty years, these facts did not appear to trouble Christians.

Everyone here probably has some familiarity (directly or indirectly) with the writings of Joseph Arthur, Comte de Gobineau. Gobineau, in his *Essay on the Inequality of the Human Races* makes clear that he believes that different races of men have been blessed by God with different attributes and that certain races of men are exclusively responsible for the creation and maintenance of high culture and civilization. I will not elaborate here on the details of Gobineau's theories since they are well known to educated persons. The important matter for me is that this author was a devout Christian, and accepted as a matter of course that, a) men, and ethnic groups of men, are not equal in their inherent abilities, and, b) that all men, from the most noble to the most primitive, have within themselves a divine spark, the *Imago Dei*, that entitles each to the special dignity reserved for children of God. Each is unique in his abilities, in the gifts that God has bestowed on him,–and this is true also of ethnic groups–but all are human and all possess a dignity appropriate to humankind.

In Gobineau's own words, "I believe, of course, that human races are unequal; but I do not think that any of them are like the brute, or to be classed with it." To the theory that some human races are simply bipedal beasts, Gobineau responds: "I absolutely reject such an insult to humanity . . . ." Comte de Gobineau served his country as a distinguished diplomat and wrote with brilliance on a wide variety of topics. Though some of his friends and some other writers disagreed with him, he was never chastised by his Church for his widely published belief in the inequality of the human races. So far as I can determine, he remained a faithful communicant of the Roman Catholic religion until his death in 1882.

Alexis Carrel, author of one of the most widely read works of nonfiction in the 1930s and 1940s, *Man the Unknown*, was also a devout Roman Catholic. Carrel was a surgeon and biologist and worked for the Rockefeller Institute for Medical Research from 1906 until his retirement in 1939. He developed methods for suturing blood vessels and did pioneering work in the field of the transplantation of organs. He won the Nobel Prize for physiology and medicine in 1912 and the Nordhoff-Jung Prize for Cancer Research in 1931. He worked with Charles Lindbergh in developing an early perfusion pump for keeping organs alive outside of the body.

Reading *Man the Unknown*, it is clear that the author entertains no notion of the equality of the human races. He writes: "Man is the hardiest of all animals, and the white races, builders of our civilization, the hardiest of all races. . . . Resistance to disease, work, and worries, capacity for effort, and nervous equilibrium are the signs of the superiority of a man. Such qualities characterized the founders of our civilization in the United States as well as in Europe. The great white races owe their success to the perfection of their nervous system–nervous system which, although very delicate and excitable, can, however, be disciplined. To the exceptional qualities of their tissues and consciousness is due the predominance over the rest of the world of the peoples of western Europe . . . ."

This forthright statement caused not the slightest ripple of controversy when it was published in 1935, nor did it do so in subsequent editions of his book published even in the immediate postwar years. As recently as that, men seemed able to discuss and debate things, and to disagree with one another, without resorting to hyperbole, *ad hominem* attacks, hysteria, and defamatory labelling. Intelligent men were still able to focus their minds on facts and issues and to think and express themselves rationally. In the 1960s, Father Joseph T. Durkin, S.J., honored the memory of Carrel in his highly laudatory biography entitled *Hope For Our Time*, in which he discusses Carrel's deep religious faith. Dr. Carrel, he writes, was a Christian believer through and through, though at times rather singular in his expressed opinions.

My third example is the Russian Orthodox sociologist and philosopher, Pitirim Sorokin, from whom I have already drawn several quotations. On the last page of Part One of John Baker's book *Race*, the author pays special tribute to Sorokin for a chapter on the racial question in Sorokin's work, *Contemporary Sociological Theories*, which appeared in 1928. About this work, Baker writes that, "Sorokin's chapter is well worth reading today, as a reminder of what was still possible before the curtain came down."

Sorokin, in this work, as well as in an earlier work entitled *Social and Cultural Mobility*, is quite frank in his discussion of various racial theories. About those theories that seek to establish the superiority of certain of the European races over other European races, the author is obviously rather dubious. Examining evidence about this, Sorokin writes that all European races "in their cultural history have shown brilliancy. . . ." On the other hand, differences in cognitive ability between Europeans and some non-Europeans, about which Sorokin discourses at considerable length, is straightforwardly acknowledged. Considering about twenty-five separate studies of the subject of IQ and race that had been completed and published up to the middle of the 1920s, Sorokin states that "the results were unanimous." They all show significant IQ differences. Sorokin concludes that, "the difference in the cultural contributions and in the historical role played by different races is excellently corroborated by, and is in perfect agreement with, the experimental studies of race mentality and psychology." That heredity is a crucial factor in the development of complex forms of civilization, Sorokin asserts, "may scarcely be questioned by any serious investigator of facts."

Now, I have mentioned two prominent Roman Catholics and one Orthodox Christian. I shall also briefly mention a Protestant Christian, Thomas Carlyle. One of the great essayists and historians of the last century, Carlyle was a Calvinist. In his early years he served as a minister of the Scottish Kirk, and though he later gave up the ministry in disagreement with certain of the dogmatic pronouncements of his Calvinist ancestors, it is written that "he was and always remained in profound sympathy with the spirit of their teachings." Anyone who knows the essays of Thomas Carlyle knows also that he was not a believer in the equality of the human races. In fact, he wrote somewhat harshly on the subject.

Now, inasmuch as he wrote on this subject at the end of the first half of the nineteenth century, perhaps his thinking is not so remarkable. Nearly all educated men, Christian or non-Christian, believed similarly at that time. But the point is that, insofar as I am aware, the published beliefs of Carlyle were not condemned at the time by the leaders of his Church. Nor, in this century, have the published beliefs of Drs. Carrel or Sorokin been condemned by the leaders of their respective Churches.

It may be argued that the evidence I have just presented in purely anecdotal and that Christian spokesmen representing the opposite viewpoint could also be assembled. Doubtless that is true. But I suppose my response to that must be that scientific findings with regard to the equality or inequality of human beings in cognitive ability in fact is not a subject on which there exists any Christian dogmatic teaching whatsoever. Though individual clergymen and members of churches may speak their minds on a variety of subjects, and may certainly disagree with one another, none may say with authority that historic Christianity possesses a dogmatic teaching on this subject of human equality or inequality. Those mainline sectarian groups that have attempted to create such dogma in recent years represent not authentic traditional Christianity, but a blend of decadent, rationalized Protestantism and Marxism.

With respect to what I have just said, I must also add a caveat that the formulation of secular, procrustean ideologies based on race, especially those which deny the innate dignity of all men, or promote the unjust or inhumane treatment of persons on account of their race, would indeed run contrary to Christian teachings and would rightly be opposed by traditional Christians.

Now, today is Sunday, and I am a priest, and priests are expected to give sermons on this day. So I have prepared a short, one or two minute sermon, in the midst of this talk, on the subject of hypocrisy.

Since the late-nineteenth century, science has grappled with the subject of racial differences and, apart from pockets of inveterate ideologues within the scientific community, it is now generally acknowledged by scientists in relevant fields that the accumulated evidence has become overwhelming that such differences do exist. (It is interesting that in 1928, Sorokin regarded the evidence as overwhelming even then.) Of particular significance have been findings related to genetically determined differences in intelligence and temperament among the various races of mankind. These are slowly coming to be accepted within scientific circles, despite formal and informal barriers now frantically being reared by Marxists, crypto-Marxists, ignorant journalists, and cowardly politicians, who love to blather on about "tolerance," "democracy," and "freedom of expression."

In many so-called free countries of the West (in Canada, for example), it is now illegal (at least to some extent) to discuss such scientific findings publicly or to publish them in most periodicals or in books. In the United States, though it is not yet illegal, those who do muster the courage to discuss such findings publicly, often find themselves subject to informal sanctions; commonplace now is character assassination in articles printed in the daily press, written by uncouth journalists–those masters of inferential falsehood. Also commonplace are threats of physical violence against the person, family, and property of the politically incorrect speaker or writer, various kinds of mob actions, and, of course, threats to the person's livelihood.

Thought control thus comes in several forms: at one end of the spectrum we have the Gulag of the old USSR, at the other end the more informal processes of thought control favored in this country, and somewhere in between the harsh laws now in force in Europe and Canada. In any case, the Orwellian intent and thug mentality are identical, only the methods and degree differ slightly. And I would add it is questionable how much worse it is being confined to a concentration camp for a thought-crime (as in the old USSR), as opposed to being ruined financially and professionally, lied about in the public press, unjustly held up to public ridicule, and subjected (along with one's family) to mob violence and terror for the same variety of thought-crime.

One would hope that in the journalistic profession a man of conscience and courage, a man of elementary decency, would occasionally step forward to remind his colleagues of their duty in a free country. Alas, (though I can think of one or two exceptions) such men seem to be almost as scarce here as in Stalin or Brezhnev's Soviet Union. Liberal journalists and their political allies justify the evil they do by pretending that they oppose what they call (in the cant of our age) "hate," "prejudice," "racism" and the like.

The plain truth is, however, that their madness has generated a sociological disaster, and human misery of appalling dimensions in the cities of the United States, primarily among racial minorities–from whom, despite their endlessly repeated slogans, the liberal journalists and politicians assiduously shield and segregate themselves and their families. Their experiments threaten in the next century to generate horrors which, by comparison, will make our current difficulties seem trifling. "Great humanitarians," these men who think of human beings as laboratory specimens! May God protect us all from their further depredations!

Even to attempt to extricate ourselves from the morass in which we now sink will require a major miracle–the renewal of our courage and of our belief in the preëminence of our way of life. The civilization of the European peoples around the globe must return to its roots if it is to accomplish that miracle, if it is, in other words, to save itself. Those roots are traditional Christianity. Father Joseph Koterski, in his recent review of the works of Christopher Dawson in *Modern Age*, states that all civilization arises out of religious belief, that culture comes from cult, and that a renewal of our commitment to traditional religion would be the "best strategy for the renewal of high culture amid the collapses of order now being experienced in a largely post-Christian era." I could not agree more.

Father Koterski goes on to make another important point: "But this is not to say with the skeptics that high culture is itself the goal and religion a more or less convenient means. . . . Rather, culture itself has a further purpose: to enable human beings progressively to discover the deepest truth about themselves as human, that their real fulfillment resides in reverence for the Transcendent God in whose image they are made." In other words, the aim of religion is not the creation of culture, but the culture it creates assists religion in achieving its ultimate goal.

Grotesque attempts have been made to obviate the need for a return to traditional Christianity by the substitution of secular ideologies. Such attempts have been catastrophic. In the last century Nietzsche postulated a coming new moral system that would replace Christianity–such systems were attempted in this century and brought about an even more dramatic erosion of the position of European man and his civilization, as well as the deaths of tens of millions of human beings in wars and revolutions. Apart from traditional Christianity, there is no alternative path, in my judgement, which will lead us to the successful revitalization of our civilization. For 2,000 years the soul of European man has been Christian. Remove that soul, and we now know that European civilization becomes sterile and, soon, dies. European civilization is Christian. If we recognize that, we begin the mighty endeavor that will lead us to renewal and renaissance.

Cৰৎষঞ

Racial Partition of the United States

Michael Hart

In the course of talking about partition of the United States, I will often be using the words "nation" and "state," so perhaps I should define them right now. The word nation refers to ethnicity. One dictionary defines a nation as: "a body of people marked off by common descent, language, culture, or historical tradition." By contrast, the word state denotes a sovereign, independent country. I will use the words "country" and "state" interchangeably. Here are some examples:

1) The Norwegians are a nation, and they have their own state, Norway.

2) The Kurds are a nation, but they do not have their own independent state.

3) Rwanda, in Africa, is a state containing two national groups, the Hutu and the Tutsi.

4) India, Nigeria, the former Soviet Union, and the former Yugoslavia are or were multinational states.

Now what should be the relationship between nations and states? Most people accept, at least in theory, the principle of self-determination, the idea that each nation or people should be allowed to choose its government, and in particular should be allowed to have its own independent country or state if desired. The principle of self-determination is closely related to the notion of democracy. Both are special cases of the general principle that, "Governments derive their just powers from the consent of the governed," which is perhaps the central notion of our Declaration of Independence.

Aside from the principle involved, there is the pragmatic consideration that most binational and multinational states do not work very well, but are beset by endless ethnic strife, often quite bloody. For example:

1) In Yugoslavia over the last few years, at least 300,000 people have died in fighting between Serbs, Croats, and Bosnian Muslims.

2) In Rwanda, during the past three years, more than 500,000 people were massacred in Hutu-Tutsi strife.

3) In Turkey, in 1915, about 1,000,000 Armenians were massacred.

4) A few years ago the Soviet Union–perhaps the largest and strongest multinational state in all of history–fell apart completely.

5) Canada, which has a much less violent history than ours, is nevertheless close to breakup.

6) The case of Cyprus is instructive: For years, there was constant fighting there between Turks and Greeks. Then, in 1974, Cyprus was invaded by Turkey, which partitioned the country into two separate states, with a more-or-less forcible exchange of populations. It was a drastic solution, but it did end the killing.

Among the many other examples of multinational states that have undergone bloody ethnic strife, I might mention India, Iraq, and Indonesia.

Why do I mention the sorry history of those multinational states? Because American blacks constitute a separate nation, which means that we ourselves are living in a multinational state. That statement may sound controversial, but the easiest way to see that it is correct is to go back to the definition of a nation. American blacks are a body of people with a common language, common descent, and a common historical tradition.

Their common language is English, which they often speak with a distinctive accent. Indeed, many of them employ a distinctive dialect called "Black English". As for common descent, they often refer to themselves as "brothers," or as "Afro-Americans," or "African-Americans". Indeed, they all do have African ancestors, mostly from sub-Saharan Africa, and specifically from West Africa.

Their common historical tradition is widely shared and deeply felt. Virtually all American blacks are familiar with the story that: (a) Their ancestors were forcibly brought to this country, where they were enslaved for centuries. (b) They were freed by the Civil War, but then suffered a century of terrible oppression under Jim Crow laws; and (c) Led by their national hero, Martin Luther King, there was a struggle for liberation in the 1960s, a struggle which was partly but not completely successful. It is worth noting that, although every nation has a historical tradition, few nations have a tradition that is as universally known and as emotionally powerful as this one.

Aside from the definition, there are many other ways in which American blacks behave as if they comprise a separate national group. Here are just a few:

1) Frequent demands for racial preferences in hiring, promotions, college admissions, etc.

2) Self-segregation on campuses, including requests for separate dormitories.

3) Formation of specifically black subgroups within most large organizations, including the American Bar Association, the American Anthropological Association, the American Museum Association, and many others.

4) Extreme bloc voting: It is common for more than 90% of blacks to vote for the same candidate in an election.

5) A separate black holiday, Kwanzaa, which was invented primarily to emphasize black separateness.

6) There is an (unofficial) black national anthem, "Lift Every Voice and Sing."

7) There is also an unofficial black national flag.

8) Many all-black private schools use a black nationalist, even separatist curriculum. For example, in one such school, instead of reciting the "Pledge of Allegiance," the children recite a "Pledge to African People." At another (the Shule Mandela Academy in East Palo Alto, California), the students pledge each morning to "think black, act black, speak black, buy black, pray black, love black, and live black."

In addition, there is a long history of black support for movements that are explicitly separatist. For example:

1) In the 1920s, Marcus Garvey, who proposed to lead American blacks back to Africa, had a few hundred thousand followers.

2) Elijah Muhammad had many followers during his 40-year reign as head of the Black Muslims.

3) And, today, Louis Farrakhan has an even larger following.

Of course, many blacks have always been loyal to the United States. Many served bravely in World War II and in other wars; many have white friends; many would like to live in an integrated society; and many feel genuine loyalty to the United States.

But, overall, even those blacks who are most loyal to the United States feel a strong identification as blacks, and have divided loyalties. Some of them identify more as Americans than as blacks; but a larger number identify more as blacks than as Americans. Of course, many blacks do not have divided loyalties, because they feel no loyalty at all to the United States! In fact, quite a few are outspokenly hostile to the United States and to the majority of its population.

The attitude of blacks to black criminals is very revealing. Many black jurors are reluctant to convict other blacks, especially if the victim is white. The most celebrated instance of this, of course, was the O.J. Simpson case: In some criminal trials the evidence is murky, but not in this one. Nevertheless, polls consistently showed that a large majority of blacks considered him not guilty, and a largely black jury acquitted him without much deliberation.

In the aftermath of the Simpson case, many whites have referred to U.S. blacks as a separate nation. For example:

1) Robert Novak, a conservative columnist, wrote: "But in private, the politicians I contacted universally agreed that . . . the Not Guilty verdict points up the nation's deepest internal problem: We are two countries, not divided between rich and poor (as Mario Cuomo has said), but between black and white."

2) Richard Cohen, who is an outspoken liberal Democrat, wrote: "We are two nations–one black, one white. Yesterday, one celebrated Simpson's acquittal, the other did not." It is hard to avoid the conclusion that this is true, and that the United States of America is indeed a multinational state.

Two Inadequate Solutions

What can be done to deal with these racial tensions? Aside from partition, there are two other plans that are often suggested. The first is usually proposed by liberal Democrats. They suggest that whites should be more strongly urged to abandon their racist attitudes, and that we need stronger civil rights laws and stronger enforcement of existing laws.

A major problem with this plan is that most American whites think that our civil rights laws have already gone too far, and they are strongly opposed to pushing reverse discrimination even further. Furthermore, even if that program were adopted, it would be ineffective. After all, a combination of civil rights laws, affirmative action programs, and endless exhortation of whites to be "less racist" has been our policy for the last 30 years, and it has obviously failed to solve our racial problems.

The other plan is quite different. It consists of the suggestion that the country should revoke its present system of "reverse discrimination" (i.e., racial preferences, quotas, and set-asides), and should instead adopt a color-blind racial policy. This plan seems much fairer; but even if it were adopted it would not work because of the intense resentment it would cause among blacks. After all, blacks are already bitterly resentful that they are "underrepresented" in colleges, in skilled occupations, and in high-paying jobs. If the present system of quotas were abandoned, blacks would hold many fewer of those jobs than they do now. This would make them even more resentful, and would result in increased black-on-white crime, including an endless series of race riots. A thorough removal of quotas is therefore unlikely.

It therefore appears that neither of those two plans can work; and in fact, it seems unlikely that any policy less drastic than partition can solve our racial problems. One strong reason for accepting this melancholy and admittedly radical conclusion is that the extensive reforms we have made during the past forty years have not come close to solving the problems. Indeed, since 1968 the situation has obviously deteriorated. Despite the elimination of all discriminatory laws against blacks, plus the adoption of numerous laws that give them positive preferences, American blacks are more angry today than they were in 1968.

Back in 1968, Malcolm X was a fringe figure, with little support. Today, Louis Farrakhan has lots of support; in fact, his "Million-Man March" in 1995 drew far more blacks than even the largest rally ever organized by Martin Luther King. Extreme anti-white rhetoric is far more prevalent today than it was 30 years ago, as is direct black-on-white violence.

Nor does the history of other multinational states provide reason for optimism. Quite the reverse: History shows that other countries that have tried to preserve unity by making large concessions to minority groups have failed to placate them. For example, in Canada, the numerous concessions made to the French-speaking minority have failed to mollify them. The French Canadians were never slaves, never had to live under "Jim Crow" laws, and have had full legal equality for well over a century. Nevertheless, in a recent vote in Quebec, 49% of the voters–and a clear majority of the French-speaking inhabitants–voted in favor of full independence for Quebec.

Another example: For most of the nineteenth century Norway and Sweden were ruled by the same king. The two nations are similar in race, language, and religion; indeed most outsiders can't even tell the difference between Norwegians and Swedes! The Norwegians were not persecuted in any way, and they had their own separate parliament and virtually complete autonomy. Still, they were not satisfied, and in 1905 declared their complete independence. Fortunately, the Swedish government was wise enough not to try to maintain unity by force.

In view of the foregoing, it seems plain that many American blacks will not be satisfied by anything less than their own independent country. Furthermore, perpetuation of the present binational state is harmful to the interests of American whites. It has caused an erosion of our traditional liberties:

1) By the widespread use of racial preferences in hiring, promotions, college admissions, etc.; and also

2) By restrictions on our freedom of speech (by means of "speech codes" on college campuses, for example).

In addition, we are victimized by high welfare costs, by high taxes, and by sky-high crime rates. (These problems are always worse in those parts of the country with large populations of blacks.) Therefore, fanciful as it may now seem to most Americans, partition of the United States is necessary. However, there is a better plan than dividing the United States into two countries.

Three-Way Partition

I propose that the United States should be divided into three separate countries: (1) an independent Black state; (2) an independent non-Black state; and (3) an integrated state.

Let me refer to the independent Black state as the "Black Separatist State," or BSS, for short. The Black Separatist State would include only those blacks who chose to become citizens of that country. It would be a fully independent country, carved out of the present territory of the United States. The size of the Black Separatist State (in property value, not in area) would be proportional to the number of people who chose to live there. Let me stress again that no blacks would be forced to live in the BSS: Citizenship in the BSS would be an option that individual blacks could choose or reject.

Let's call the independent non-black state the "White Separatist State," or WSS (although it might include some Asians and others.) Like the BSS, the White Separatist State would include only those individuals who chose to become citizens. It would be a fully independent country, carved out of the present territory of the United States. The size of the WSS (in value, not in area) would be proportional to the number of people who originally chose to live there. Again, I wish to stress that citizenship in the WSS would be an option; nobody would be forced to live there.

The third country, the integrated state, would be a continuation of the present United States of America, but with a reduced area. All American citizens who did not explicitly choose to become citizens of the BSS or the WSS would remain members of the integrated USA. Therefore, just after the partition, the tangible wealth of the integrated USA would be proportional to the number of people who chose to remain its citizens.

Advantages of Three-Way Partition

Although a three-way partition is more complicated than a two-way plan, it has three great advantages:

1) It is more fair;

2) It is more advantageous for the separatists than a two-way partition; and

3) It would be easier to get approved.

As for fairness, it is plain that partition is fairer to black separatists than the present system is. Many American blacks now feel aggrieved that they do not have their own country. They know that blacks living here today are a minority–probably a permanent minority–and they therefore feel that they cannot control their own destiny. And they are right! Black Americans are one of the largest national groups in the whole world who do not have their own independent country.

Partition is also fairer to white separatists than the present system. Many whites feel that their country is being taken away from them.

1) They are losing their rights.

2) They are losing their personal safety.

3) Their traditions are no longer respected and protected.

4) And, worst of all, if there is no change in immigration policy we will soon be a permanent minority in what used to be our country. We therefore quite naturally want to preserve a separate country for ourselves.

Now either a two-way partition of the United States or a three-way division would satisfy most separatists. However, a three-way division is fairer to integrationists than any two-way plan could possibly be. Many whites really want to live in an integrated society. They would be horrified at the prospect of living in a white separatist state, which they would regard as "fascist". A two-way partition plan would be unfair to them. It would also be unfair to those blacks who really want integration and do not want to live in a country dominated by Louis Farrakhan or any similar leader.

We don't want integrationists to prevent us from choosing to live in a separate white state. In fairness, then, we should not deprive them of their choice to live in a racially integrated state, no matter how foolish we think their choice may be. At present, integrationists are imposing their notion of fairness on everyone else, but why should their desires be given preference to those of black separatists? Or of white separatists? In a two-way partition, separatists would be forcing their way on integrationists, but in a three-way partition, everyone gets to live in the country of his choice.

The second important reason why we should prefer a three-way partition plan is that white separatists would be much better off in a three-way split than we would be if the United States were divided into only two countries, one white and one black. If there were only two countries, the white state would necessarily start off with a large, disgruntled, embittered minority, consisting of those whites who were opposed to partition, which would cause tremendous internal problems. Remember: Those who favor partition are in the minority right now, and no partition plan can be implemented until a majority of the American public is willing to accept it. We must therefore be willing to delay partition for 20 or 30 years while we gain more public support for the idea. Therefore, at the time partition were adopted–shortly after the proposal gained majority support–only 55% or 60% of the public would support it.

Under those circumstances, if the country is partitioned into two states, the white state will start off bitterly divided into two factions, which is a recipe for disaster, especially since one of those factions would be opposed to the very existence of that state. However, in a three-way division, the White Separatist State would start off with a population that is basically united on racial attitudes and on the desirability of partition, which would greatly increase its chances of functioning successfully.

There is another reason why whites would be better off with a three-way split: In a three-way partition, the white state is likely to end up with the lion's share of the most productive citizens. This would happen because everyone would expect the White Separatist State to have a basically conservative government. Therefore, most whites who favor the policies of the "liberal Democrats" (i.e., a generous welfare policy, "big government," and high taxes), would probably choose to remain citizens of the integrated state. Similarly, most people would expect the integrated state to be dominated by liberal Democrats. Therefore, most whites who favor "conservative" policies (such as reduced welfare, "small government," and lower taxes) would probably choose to live in the White Separatist State. People's expectations in this regard would probably become self-fulfilling. With more conservatives than liberals choosing the white state, those who remained behind in the integrated state would include a disproportionate number of liberals and welfare recipients. And with most liberals choosing the integrated state, the White Separatist State would indeed have a relatively conservative government, and would attract many entrepreneurs, professionals, skilled workers, and other highly productive citizens. As a result, over a 30- to 50-year time span the integrated United States would probably become an advanced "welfare state," like Sweden, and stagnate economically, whereas the white state would become a comparatively "laisser- faire," capitalist state like Singapore, Switzerland, Hong Kong, or the 19th-century United States, and become much more prosperous.

The third major advantage of a three-way partition is that it would be much easier to get it approved than a two-way division. It is clear that those people (of any race) who prefer to live in an integrated country will strenuously oppose any two-way partition plan; however, some of those people would agree to a three-way partition which, indeed, they might well think was an improvement on the present state of affairs.

After all, the way they look at it, their goal of a just, integrated society with little or no racial tensions is being thwarted by the opposition of die-hard white segregationists and black extremists, such as the followers of Louis Farrakhan. Therefore, in their view, if the white and black extremists were to leave, the remaining population would consist of those persons (of both races) who favor integration, and are committed to it. Integrationists should therefore anticipate that the integrated state remaining after a three-way partition would have much lower racial tensions than today's United States. It should therefore be much easier to gain their assent to a three-way partition than to a two-way plan.

In addition, many people with a libertarian outlook are likely to support a three-way partition because it maximizes the choices available to individuals, even though they might oppose a two-way division.

Details of the Plan

By what procedure could a three-way partition of the United States be carried out? In particular, how would the boundaries of the three countries be determined? As I said before, partition cannot be carried out now; more popular support is needed. Furthermore, the Constitution as it now stands does not provide for or permit partition. Therefore, a Constitutional amendment would be needed, which would cause more delay.

Since partition is at least 20 years away, it is clearly premature to try to specify all the details of how it would be carried out. However, in order to make my discussion less abstract, I will outline one possible method. I do not wish to imply that this is the only possible method, or necessarily the best method.

In the plan I am suggesting, partition would be implemented in four stages. In the first stage, each adult would tentatively choose which of the three countries he or she wishes to join. Of course, whites could not become citizens of the black state, nor could blacks join the White Separatist State; but anyone would be free to choose the integrated state. In the second stage, a special committee would be formed to draw up tentative boundaries for the three states. The members of this special committee–lets call it the "Boundary Committee," or BC, for short–would be selected by Congress. The BC would not draw boundaries arbitrarily, but rather in accordance with specific criteria laid out by Congress. For example:

1) The tangible wealth of the three countries should be roughly proportional to their initial populations;

2) Each of the three countries should have a wide variety of resources, such as farm land, minerals, factories, roads, railways, and ports.

3) If possible, each country should be a single, connected, compact territory.

3) As much as possible (consistent with the foregoing) the least number of people should need to move in order to be in the country of their choice.

After drawing tentative boundaries based on the stage one voting, the Boundary Committee would then draw up sets of alternative boundary lines to be used if the relative populations of the three states change significantly in the next stage of the partition.

During the third stage of the partition, after the Boundary Committee has issued its report and published its maps, there would be a six-month period during which each citizen would have the opportunity to revise the choice he or she made during the first stage. At the end of that six-month period, the individual choices become final, and the populations of the three states would be tallied. On the basis of that tally, the final boundaries would be announced, in accordance with the maps drawn by the Boundary Committee during stage two.

The fourth and final stage of the partition would involve the actual movement of people. This would take place over a one- or two-year interval. People who moved would be compensated by the government for their property, and for their relocation expenses. Each of the three governments would thereby acquire a lot of residential property, which it would then auction off to its own citizens.

It is plain that the citizens of the black state would gain financially in this process, since American blacks now own much less than their proportional share of the total wealth of the United States. Since blacks would gain in the process, and since the partition would not in the short run create any tangible wealth, it seems plain that the integrated state and the White Separatist State would each lose money during the partition. They might agree to share this net expense proportionately.

At the end of the partition, the three states would be three completely independent countries. They would not be required to accept immigrants or visitors from the others, nor to trade with the others. However, as a practical matter, the three states would probably permit ordinary trade and tourism (although perhaps with some restrictions), and the three states might join in some sort of "common market."

Conclusion

As you can see, a three-way partition is much more complicated than a two-way partition. Just solutions to problems usually are complicated, because life is complicated, and human relations are complicated. But it is much better to have a complicated plan than one that is simple, but unfair. Furthermore, it would be more difficult to get an unfair plan accepted.

There is one more problem: As I pointed out before, a partition of the United States cannot be carried out right now. We will have to wait quite a few years before this goal is achieved. That is a problem that all political minorities face: Their ideas cannot be adopted immediately, unless they are able and willing to use violence to force their views on an unwilling majority, which I think is a terrible idea. Quite the contrary, we should do everything we can to avert violence.

Indeed, a major problem with the present situation is that it involves continual low-level racial violence, and the possibility that racial tensions will erupt into major violence cannot be ignored. Indeed, major violence between ethnic groups has occurred in many other binational or multinational states. We don't want it to happen here.

A race war in the United States would be a horrible disaster for everyone. My partition plan has been designed to avert bloodshed by giving everyone–blacks and whites alike–the opportunity to get most of what they want without violence. Let us hope that is what happens.

CR80

Diversity in the Human Genome

Glayde Whitney

There is a revolution taking place around us. It is a conceptual revolution driven by scientific knowledge. Its impact on mankind will be greater than that of the Copernican revolution or the Darwinian revolution. Its factual basis is knowledge of man's genetic nature. This revolution–it can be called the Galtonian revolution–stands a fair chance of revolutionizing what we know about race. It sounds the death knell of politically correct egalitarianism as we know it today.

The Galtonian revolution got off to a bit of a slow start in the 1860's when Francis Galton began his epoch-making studies of human individual differences, heredity and behavior. It was he who named the famous bell-curve statistical distribution a "normal" distribution. It was Galton who invented methods of analysis, such as regressions and correlations, in order to understand human heredity, and it was Galton who first uttered the phrase "nature versus nurture," and coined the term "eugenics." But the biology of heredity–the chemistry of units later called genes–was not understood until well into the twentieth century (Whitney, 1990).

Until very recently most of our knowledge about genetics consisted of deductions from patterns of inheritance of traits among family members, and statistical inferences from traits in populations. We have known very little about the actual molecular chemistry of inheritance. This lack of knowledge has resulted in never-ending arguments about the causes of race differences.

For example, it is widely accepted among scientists (although rarely acknowledged in public) that blacks and whites differ substantially in average IQ. The never-ending arguments hinge on whether the cause of the difference is genetic or environmental. Over the last 40 years both environmentalists and hereditarians have generally agreed that an adoption study would settle the question. If black children, adopted and reared in middle-class white families, grew up to function intellectually and emotionally like whites it would be a strong argument for environment. If they grew up to function like blacks it would establish that the race differences were largely genetic.

The study has been done (Scarr and Weinberg 1976, Weinberg, Scarr and Waldman 1992) and the results are clear: By the time they are young adults, blacks who have been raised in bright, white, middle-class homes and school environments show virtually no benefit from the experience; their average IQ is not raised. This is clear evidence for the hereditarian position, but it has not stopped the debate (Levin, 1994; Lynn, 1994; Waldman, et al, 1994; Whitney, 1996). Environmentalists simply reinterpret the evidence as indicating that outside-the-home societal prejudices hinder black IQ even more than anyone expected!

Arguments over interpretation can continue only because we lack molecular knowledge of the genes that influence IQ (except for a few rare abnormal mutations), and therefore do not know the distribution of such genes among the races. Only in the last few decades have scientific breakthroughs occurred in our techniques for studying genes at the molecular level. We are actually now beginning to read the genetic blueprint. Coordinated projects have been designed to discover all the genes that comprise *Homo sapiens*, in what may be one of the most portentous scientific efforts ever conceived. When the study–known as the Human Genome Project–is complete, we will not have the answers to all our questions but the genetic Rosetta Stone will have been decoded (Lander, 1996). Today we know so little that we cannot even speculate about what we will find written in the genes, but we will finally be able to read what is there.

Along the way to the ultimate goal, there are a number of interim goals. These involve finding what are called genetic markers, and putting together genetic maps. Projects of this kind are also going on for useful other species like mice and fruit flies, which are model organisms for research. In order to understand some of these endeavors, we need to understand some basic genetic terms and concepts. Readers may skip to the section "Whose Genome" if they wish, but they will understand the genome project much better if they are aware of some of the underlying science.

Genetics

Genes govern every detail of every structure and function of every cell in the human body. Although they operate in constant interaction with the environment, genes control every physiological function, from growth to healing to digestion to data-processing in the brain–and they do so from conception to death. A tremendous amount of information–the entire biological blueprint for each individual human being–is contained in the genes.

The material in which this information is stored is *DNA*, or deoxyribonucleic acid. Humans have 23 separate but very long strings of DNA, which are called *chromosomes*. *Genes*, of which there are an estimated 50,000 to 100,000, are distinct portions of the DNA, and are arranged along the 23 different chromosomes.

The components of DNA that *code* or record the genetic blueprint are called *bases* (because their chemical nature is alkaline, or basic, rather than acidic). There are only four different bases, adenine (A), guanine (G), cytosine (C), and thymine (T). They can be thought of as letters in the chemical alphabet that is used to record the details of the genetic blueprint. Just as the 26 letters of our alphabet are combined in different sequences to make different words with different meanings, the four bases are arranged in different sequences that indicate every detail of what a cell does and what chemical products it makes.

The "words" in this chemical language of bases can be very long. Each gene consists of a region of DNA (located on one of the chromosomes) that ranges in length from a sequence of a few thousand bases to over one hundred thousand bases. The complete set of this information about a species or individual is called its *genome*. The DNA of the human genome consists of a sequence of about *3 billion* bases. If this material were stretched out straight, it would be about three feet long, but the DNA is helixed and folded and refolded into chromosomes that fit within the microscopic nucleus of a single cell!

If the four letters of the DNA code (A,T,G,C), were printed in small type, it would take about 200,000 pages of print to specify the genome. It would take the equivalent of 200 Manhattan telephone books of 1,000 pages each to record all the genetic information contained in the nucleus of every human cell. Of those 200,000 pages, we now know the exact sequence of bases for about 200 pages, or one inch out of the three feet. And that one inch is in bits and pieces scattered throughout the genome rather than in one place. The longest continuous sequence (at least until recently) was 865,000 bases long; perhaps one-fourth of a millimeter (Mansfield, 1996). The purpose of the Human Genome Project is to locate and identify (or *sequence*, as the scientists say) all three billion bases.

A gene is a length of DNA where a specific sequence of bases acts as the code used to build a specific functional product for the body, usually a polypeptide or protein. These functional products are the building blocks of the body and are the ingredients of the body's myriad chemical processes. The procedure for building these products is called *translation* or *transcription*, because the information in the gene is processed sequentially, base by base, to make something the body needs. It is these gene products, and the interactions among the products of many genes, that constitute the chemical and observable characteristics that make a person.

The position on a chromosome where a particular gene exists is called its *locus*. For example, at one locus there might be a gene that codes for eye pigment, causing its bearer to be blue-eyed. An alteration of the base sequence at that locus (a mutation) might change the gene to one causing the eyes to be brown. Each different form of the gene at that locus is called an *allele*. Many genes are exactly the same in all people, so there is only one form of the gene. All people have an enormous number of body functions and structures in common, and that portion of their genetic code is therefore the same. Other genes have alternative forms and therefore account for (or cause) human differences. A gene with more than one alternative form, or allele, that is common in a population (*any* gene can have rare, mutant forms, but they do not become common if the bearers do not survive) is said to be *polymorphic*. A population consisting of many people could have many different alternative alleles of any particular polymorphic gene.

Cell Division and Reproduction

Every DNA molecule is actually composed of two paired strands or sequences of bases. The strands are held together by chemical attraction between the bases, in a physical form that resembles the way the steps of a ladder hold the two sides together (see figure). In forming the steps, the bases on one strand always pair with the bases on the other stand in a specific way: T always pairs with A, and G always pairs with C. Thus the two strands contain two complementary versions of the same genetic information.

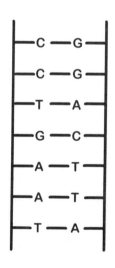

When a cell is going to divide and the DNA is to be copied, the two sides of the DNA molecule separate, as if they were unzipped, and each strand serves as a template for building the complementary strand. All the cell needs to do is pair every A with a T and every C with a G, and the two DNA strands can be duplicated. When the cell divides, each of the two daughter cells thus gets an exact duplicate of the DNA from the parent cell. It is the chemical specificity of base pairing–T always to A, G always to C–that allows the body to make exact copies of its genes and thus maintain structural and functional coherence. This is *self-replication*, one of the fundamental properties of life.

(Cells make exact copies *most* of the time. *Mutations* are a wide variety of changes that can occur. An incorrect base may be substituted during the copying process, or a base pair may be skipped. A region of DNA may be duplicated or deleted, or moved from one place to another. Many alterations in fine and gross structure are possible, but they are rare).

Since gene loci are arranged along 23 chromosomes, it could have been the case that all genes were inherited as 23 "linked" sets. All traits would have been *assorted*, or arranged, into 23 categories that were inherited together. However, a special kind of cell division takes place when the reproductive cells are formed, and the genetic material originally received from the (grand)parents is thoroughly mixed before it goes into an egg or sperm.

The mother includes one copy of her genome in the egg and the father one copy of his in the sperm. With the exception of the sex-determining y chromosome, which comes from the father and results in a boy, the child therefore gets two copies of each chromosome, one from each parent, for a total of 46. If the two copies have genes with the same alleles (such as the code for blue eyes) the individual is said to be *homozygous*. If the alleles are different (one for blue, one for brown) the individual is *heterozygous*. An individual's genetic complement is his *genotype*.

If we consider just one locus with two possible alleles (A1 and A2), there are three possible genotypes: two homozygous (A1A1 and A2A2) and one heterozygous (A1A2). Among humans there is an astronomical number of possible genotypes. For instance, imagine just one locus with 20 possible alleles: There are 20 homozygous genotypes in addition to 190 heterozygous ones ($[\{20\}\{19\}]/2 = 190$) for a total of 210. With just four such loci, the number of possible combinations (genotypes) is 210 to the 4th power, or about 2 billion. With only five loci, the possible genotypes are more than 400 billion, a figure that far exceeds the current world population of less than seven billion. Of course, the human genome does not consist of 4 or 5 loci but something on the order of 50,000 to 100,000 genes. The number of different possible humans is therefore a number so large that the human mind can scarcely grasp it.

New genes are being discovered and mapped to a precise location on a chromosome all the time. A December 8, 1996 check of the Johns Hopkins on-line depository of human genetic data, "GenBank," listed 8,271 entries for genes. It is possible to be sure of the existence of a gene without knowing exactly where on the DNA chain it is located, so a gene locus was known for only 5,310 of the 8,271. This is a very small percentage of 100,000, but in 1958 only 412 human genes were known, and most of them were not mapped to a definite locus. Every year we know more than we did the year before (Schuler, et. al, 1996; Rowen, Mahairas, & Hood, 1997).

Whose Genome?

Since every person's genotype is different, exactly which 3 billion or so base pairs are being mapped? The standard answer is that a "representative genome" is going to be completely sequenced and it will be the standard against which to compare chunks sequenced from particular individuals–mutations of medical interest, for example.

The representative genome was supposed to be a composite from a diversity of sources–anonymous donors who had given informed consent. In practice, most of the initial material came from three men and one woman, not completely anonymous and not with informed consent. Much of the material was ejaculate from a scientist working on the project.

The folks who worry about public relations and "ethics" became very concerned, because "elitist" ejaculate wouldn't do. Feminists wanted women equally represented despite the fact that you cannot get a complete human genome sequence from women because normal women have no y chromosome. The problem went all the way to the top and the sequencing part of the project had to start over with sample DNA from a suitably diverse assortment of non-elite anonymous donors who gave informed consent (Marshall, 1996).

In fact, it would have been interesting to have completely sequenced the genome of a single, known person. Knowledge of his genotype could have been compared with what was known of the person. But this would presumably have implied that there was an "ideal" person to whom all others were being compared.

Maps and Markers

One part of the Human Genome Project has been establishment of a genetic linkage map. Informative landmarks, or marker loci, have been determined at approximately equal intervals along the entire genome. The loci used are called "markers," rather than genes, because the DNA is "silent" at these places, that is to say, it does not actually code for any known function or cell product. In fact, much of the genome is made up of this silent, "anonymous DNA." Some people believe that this is excess baggage, perhaps left over from ancient evolutionary experiments. Others suspect it has important functions of which we are simply ignorant.

Many of these markers, or landmarks, are short, simple repeats of DNA base sequences with variations in the number of repeating sequences. The markers are used in procedures to help locate more complex, functional genes. Some are highly polymorphic, that is, a large number of different alleles exist for them. Besides providing an outline map for the genome, they also have a very interesting forensic use, and their patterns of occurrence provide important data about racial differences.

Comparing markers in genetic samples from different individuals is the essence of "DNA fingerprinting," or profiling, a forensic technique that is only about ten years old, but has already become very important. This procedure can distinguish between individuals with 100 percent accuracy. Also, because different alleles for different marker loci consistently appear with different frequencies in different races and subraces, ethnic identification is also 100 percent accurate.

A pre-publication copy of a 1996 U.S. National Research Council Report called *The Evaluation of Forensic DNA Evidence* (National Research Council, 1966) reported:

> DNA analysis promises to be the most important tool for human identification since Francis Galton developed the use of fingerprints for that purpose. We can confidently predict that, in the not-distant future, persons as closely related as brothers will be routinely distinguished, and DNA profiles will be as fully accepted as fingerprints now are . . . . (from the Preface)

The population of the United States is made up of subpopulations descended from different parts of the globe and not fully homogenized. . . . Extensive studies from a wide range of databases show that there are indeed substantial frequency differences [in marker alleles] among the major racial and linguistic groups (black, Hispanic, American Indian, east Asian, and white). . . . The main reason for departures from random-mating proportions in forensic DNA markers is population structure due to incomplete mixing of ancestral stocks." (p. O-20).

In other words, for as long as Americans are *not* a completely interbred people with precisely equal percentages of ancestors from every race, their DNA will always record the differences. For example, various marker alleles occur with different frequencies in individuals of different European stocks. Using such alleles in appropriate prediction equations, it could be quite straightforward correctly to identify a particular white American as being of, for instance, mixed Celtic (Irish), Nordic (Swedish) and Mediterranean (Italian) ancestry. Some subpopulations, such as various American Indian tribes, differ very substantially from each other in marker composition.

Genetic marker diversity can be used to investigate the veracity of oral traditions. Members of the Lemba, a black Bantu-speaking South African tribe, have an oral tradition that they are descended from Semitic, Jewish or Muslim, traders. One version of the tribal myth is that their ancestors included pre-Christian-era Jewish traders stranded in Africa when their base city was sacked. The Lemba maintain the myth as well as some cultural practices, such as ritual slaughter of animals and male circumcision, which are not common among their Bantu neighbors. Genetic markers support the tradition. Common among Lemba men are y-chromosome gene markers that are also common among Semites but rare in other blacks (Lewin, 1997).

Even at this very early stage of genomic analysis, in which polymorphic markers are used for identification, it has already become obvious that there are substantial genetic differences between the races. It is trivial to identify *unerringly* the race of any individual, including mixes of various races (Shriver, et al, 1997). This fact should forever dispel the myth of racial equivalence. Fashionable nonsense to the effect that race is a social rather than a biological phenomenon is clearly and demonstrably false. Advocates of a socialist utopia founded on egalitarian fallacy are justifiably terrified of the genome project, because the possibilities for obfuscation and denial are being severely limited.

The Percent Scams

Knowledge from the genome project has already helped put in perspective some previously misunderstood, or intentionally misrepresented, genetic information–what I call the "percent scams." There have been two main scams, one at one percent, another at six percent. The one-percent scam started from genuine surprise among scientists at the similarity in base sequences between early samples of chimp and human DNA. In some comparisons it appeared that we shared about 99 percent of our genetic material with the chimpanzee (King & Wilson, 1975), and egalitarian anthropologists immediately exploited this similarity. If there is only one percent of difference between the two species, it must follow that all men are genetically functionally equivalent. By this "proof," racial differences must be due to historical accident and cultural differentiation–not genetic differentiation–since there is no room for genetic differentiation (Washburn, 1978).

Better understanding of the genome reveals that "percent difference," is not a relevant comparison. Small differences can matter tremendously. Mice and humans, for example, have many DNA sequences in common, and many mouse genes are very similar to human genes. It takes a lot of the same genetic blueprint to build mammalian bodies with liver, spleen, digestive tract, skeletal systems, and nervous systems. And, in fact, there are many similarities between mouse and man, as any anatomy student can verify by direct examination. There are also important differences.

With apes we share many of our genes. However, we could share 99 percent of our base pair sequences and still differ in 100 percent of our gene products, depending on how the one percent difference were distributed throughout the genome (Plomin & Kuse, 1979). Since genes and protein products interact in complex ways, often small differences in genes can cascade to enormous differences in final traits.

As an example, consider that among humans the manifold differences between the sexes are, on present evidence, the result of a difference in *only one gene*. The gene in question is a regulatory gene, that is, its primary product interacts with the DNA to regulate the expression of many other genes. With the *tdf* gene (testes determining factor, also known as Sry, or the Sex determining Region of the y chromosome) you get a male; without the *tdf* gene, a female (Haqq, et al, 1994). Sry is only one gene out of 50,000 to 100,000. The argument that the "only one percent difference" between ape and man is evidence for genetic identity among humans can now only be maintained as a deliberate scam.

The six percent scam began in 1972 with Richard Lewontin. He is the brilliant Harvard biologist who co-authored (with Leon Kamin and Steven Rose) the Marxist screed *Not in Our Genes*. In the early days of population comparisons of allelic patterns, Lewontin (1972) catalogued the frequencies across seven racial groups for 29 alleles from 17 gene loci, from which he calculated a statistical genetic diversity index. He reported that 85.4 percent of the genetic diversity was contained within local populations, an additional 8.3 percent of the diversity was between populations within a race, and only 6.3 percent of the genetic diversity differentiated the major races. (These are percentages of Lewontin's index, and not percentages of genes, so the numbers are not comparable to the percentage of genes shared by humans and chimps.) Other investigators have reported similar results. From the finding that only about six percent of the diversity differentiated the major races, Lewontin ended his 1972 paper with the politically correct non sequitur that:

> Human racial classification is of no social value and is positively destructive of social and human relations. Since such racial classification is now seen to be of virtually no genetic or taxonomic significance either, no justification can be offered for its continuance. (Lewontin, 1972, p. 397).

That paper and its conclusion became a classic in the egalitarian armamentarium but the Lewontin argument is a scam in the same way the Chimpanzee comparison is a scam. The fact that there is much genetic diversity among people within local populations is very important. However, the meaningful question about racial differences is not the percentage of total diversity, but rather how the diversity is distributed among the races, what traits it influences, and how it is patterned.

It has indeed been a surprise to many geneticists to discover how much genetic diversity there is in local populations. Two brothers, for example, share fully half their alleles by descent, but differ in countless ways. According to Lewontin's statistical formulation they account for much genetic diversity just between the two of them.

Nevertheless, to understand how meaningless this approach is as an analysis of racial differences, one might consider the extent to which humans and macaque monkeys share genes and alleles. If the total genetic diversity of humans *plus* macaques is given an index of 100 percent, *more than half* of that diversity will be found in a troop of macaques or in the population of Belfast. This does *not* mean Irishmen differ more from their neighbors than they do from macaques–which is what the Lewontin approach slyly implies.

Patterned Diversity

Since the mid-1980s there have been a number of population surveys looking at genetic diversity, and virtually all the serious ones find the same racial patterning. The thousand-page tome published in 1994 by L. Luca Cavalli-Sforza and his colleagues (*The History and Geography of Human Genes*) is one of the better known. They present 491 world populations using data for 128 alleles at 45 polymorphic loci. The populations are grouped in various meaningful ways, aggregated into 42 populations, which are combined into nine clusters.

Cavalli-Sforza *et. al.* are adamant that they are not studying races, but rather populations of humans. However, their nine clusters have a familiar ring: "Africans (sub-Saharan), Caucasoids (European) . . . Northern Mongoloids (excluding Arctic populations) . . . ." (1994, p.79) The figure below presents a graphic schematization of their major findings with regard to patterning of genetic diversity. In their words, from their genetic data, "the greatest difference within the human species is between Africans and non-Africans . . . . The cluster formed by Caucasoids, northern Mongoloids, and Amerinds is reasonably compact in all analyses." (1994, p. 83) Thus, from investigation of gene distributions not only are the races and major subraces of man clustered, but also the relative degree of genetic difference reflects the degree of differences observed for traits such as intelligence and criminality–sub-Saharan Africans are most different from all other humans.

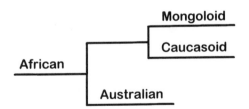

Another frequency survey was reported by the noted geneticists M. Nei and A.K. Roychoudhury (1993), who looked at the distribution of 121 alleles of 29 genes for 26 population samples. Arthur Jensen (in press) then subjected the data to factor analysis with varimax rotation, a procedure that reveals which variables cluster together. With his kind permission, the results, which are to be published in his forthcoming book, *The g Factor*, are presented in the table on the next page.

The results show that by standard statistical procedures the genetic data from the 26 populations yield six components that show which populations cluster together most distinctly. The size of a numerical entry indicates how close a particular population is to the central tendency of a cluster. The dashes indicate values of less than 200, which have been left out for clarity.

Notice that some populations have a major loading on one component and a minor loading on another; these represent combinations of genetic clusters. The six components reflect clusters that are easily identified as the following population groups: (1) Mongoloids, (2) Caucasoids, (3) South Asians and Pacific Islanders, (4) Negroids, (5) North and south Amerindians plus Eskimos, (6) aboriginal Australians and Papuan New Guineans. These genetically defined components are *racial groupings* quite similar to the population groups obtained in the Cavalli-Sforza study mentioned above. More importantly, these two examples illustrate that modern genetic diversity studies are converging on a human population structure that is amazingly similar to racial classifications suggested by classical physical anthropologists such as Carleton Coon, whose work has been thoroughly abused by a recent generation of politically correct scholars. These data are therefore a virtually irrefutable demonstration of the reality of race–a purely statistical analysis of allele frequencies gives results that are essentially identical to the racial groupings established by traditional anthropology (see also Miller, 1994).

The Genomic Future

The eminent human geneticist T. E. Reed (personal communication) has pointed out that we know almost nothing about the racial apportionment of human genetic diversity. Indeed only about five percent of the approximately 100,000 human genes have even been characterized, and only a few hundred have been used in population surveys. "What is known about the distribution of the other 99-plus percent of loci? Nothing!" he reminds us.

Unless censorship is imposed, we will soon be unable to avoid many truths. The range of possibilities is enormous. It is possible that the "only-skin-deep," observable differences between the major races will turn out to be the tips of some very differentiated icebergs. Great genetic differentiation is suggested by the data summarized on the

**Components of a Genetic Similarity Matrix for 26 Populations
(Values less than 200 omitted for clarity).**

Varimax Rotated Components

Population	1	2	3	4	5	6
Pygmy	–	–	–	651	–	–
Nigerian	–	–	–	734	–	–
Bantu	–	–	–	747	–	–
San (Bushman)	–	–	–	465	–	–
Lapp	–	500	–	–	–	–
Finn	–	988	–	–	–	–
German	–	978	–	–	–	–
English	–	948	–	–	–	–
Italian	–	989	–	–	–	–
Iranian	–	635	–	–	–	–
North Indian	–	704	–	–	–	–
Japanese	936	–	214	–	–	–
Korean	959	–	229	–	–	–
Tibetan	855	–		–	–	–
Mongolian	842	–	357	–	–	–
Southern Chinese	331	–	771	–	–	–
Thai	–	–	814	–	–	–
Filipino	–	–	782	–	–	–
Indonesian	–	–	749	–	–	–
Polynesian	–	–	526	–	–	284
Micronesian	–	–	521	–	–	328
Australian (aborigines)	–	–	–	–	–	706
Papuan (New Guineans)	–	–	–	–	–	742
North Amerindian	–	–	–	–	804	–
South Amerindian	–	–	–	–	563	–
Eskimo	–	–	–	–	726	–

Adapted from Arthur Jensen's Table 12.N in MS of *The g Factor*.

previous page. The human species, with its geographically distinct ancestral populations, may have much more patterned diversity than is commonly appreciated.

For example, what constitutes a genetic species? Lions and tigers, when brought together artificially, are capable of interbreeding, as are wolves, dogs, and coyotes. Humanity is indeed diverse and polygenic, and we will soon have the tools to know to what extent. It could easily be found that there is far more consistent genetic difference between the different races–all thought to be the same species–than there is between wolves and coyotes, for example, which can interbreed but are recognized as distinct species.

The Human Genome Project, even if completed on schedule in 2005, will not answer all our questions. Rather it will provide a framework within which, for the first time, it will be feasible and efficient to seek the answers. Much more physiological and psychological work remains to be done, and partial sequences will have to be gathered from many different individuals and races. However, for the first time we will be able to answer questions of great importance: What is human nature? Or rather, what are human natures? Why are some human groups statistically so very different for so many traits?

The "nature versus nurture" problem will be solved. The differentiation of the sexes, as well as the developmental revolutions that separate children from adults will also be understood with a completeness far beyond earlier comprehension. And to understand the origin of the kinds of racially differentiated traits catalogued by J. Philippe Rushton (1995) in *Race, Evolution, and Behavior*, modern science will be able to go beyond statistics, supposition, and ideology to definitive biological answers.

The ideologues of egalitarianism are well aware of these possibilities, and are already trying to block research and even discussion (Lamb, 1994; Pearson, 1997; Whitney, 1996, 1997). "Hate speech" laws are being tightened in many countries, and discussion of race differences can get you fired or bring criminal charges in France, Germany, Canada, and Australia. In the United States, researchers routinely censor themselves and their "insensitive" colleagues, for fear of losing jobs or funding (Plomin & Petrill, 1997). Knowledge could be driven underground even more than it is today, but if science is unfettered we are on the verge of great new discoveries.

Until the previous century, chemists worked with the elements of air, earth, fire, and water. It was only with the establishment of the periodic table of elements that anyone could have imagined modern plastics or silicon-gallium computer chips. The Human Genome Project is discovering the *human* elements, and the consequences are likely to be just as profound and unanticipated.

References

Cavalli-Sforza, L. L., Menozzi, P., & Piazza, A. (1994) *The History and Geography of Human Genes.* Princeton NJ: Princeton University Press.

Haqq, C. M., King, C-Y., Ukiyama, E., Falsafi, S., Haqq, T. N., Donahoe, P. K., & Weiss, M. A. (1994) Molecular basis of mammalian sexual determination: Activation of Mullerian inhibiting substance gene expression by SRY. *Science, 266,* 1494-1500.

Jensen, A. (in press) *The g Factor.* New York: Praeger.

King, M. C., & Wilson, A. C. (1975) Evolution at two levels in humans and chimpanzees. *Science, 188,* 107-116.

Lamb, K. (1994) Race differences in the annals of science. *The Mankind Quarterly, 35,* 139-150.

Lander, E. S. (1996) The new genomics: Global views of biology. *Science, 274,* 536-539.

Levin, M. (1994) Comment on the Minnesota transracial adoption study. *Intelligence, 19,* 13-20.

Lewin, D. I. (1997) Barking up the Lemba family tree with DNA polymorphisms. *The Journal of NIH Research, 9,* 33-35.

Lewontin, R. C. (1972) The apportionment of human diversity. In: Dobzhansky, T., Hecht, M. K., & Steere, W. C. (Eds.), *Evolutionary Biology, Vol. 6,* New York: Appleton Century Crofts, Pp. 381-398.

Lewontin, R. C., Rose, S., & Kamin, L. J. (1984) *Not in Our Genes.* New York: Pantheon.

Lynn, R. (1994) Some reinterpretations of the Minnesota transracial adoption study. *Intelligence, 19,* 21-27.

Mansfield, B. K. (1996) (Managing Editor), *Human Genome News, 8, #1,* ISSN: 1050-6101. U.S. Department of Energy.

Marshall, E. (1996) Whose genome is it, anyway? *Science, 273,* 1788-1789.

Miller, E. M. (1994) Tracing the genetic history of modern man: A review. *The Mankind Quarterly, 35,* 71-108.

National Research Council (1996) *The Evaluation of Forensic DNA Evidence.* Prepublication Copy. Washington DC: National Academy Press.

Nei, M., & Roychoudhury, A. K. (1993) Evolutionary relationships of human populations on a global scale. *Molecular Biology and Evolution, 10,* 927-943.

Pearson, R. (1997) *Race, Intelligence and Bias in Academe.* 2nd *Ed.* Washington DC: Scott-Townsend.

Plomin, R., & Kuse, A. R. (1979) Comment in response to S. L. Washburn: Human behavior and the behavior of other organisms. *American Psychologist, 34,* 188-190.

Plomin, R., & Petrill, S. A. (1997) Genetics and intelligence: What's new? *Intelligence, 24,* 53-77.

Rowen, L., Mahairas, G., & Hood, L. (1997) Sequencing the human genome. *Science, 278,* 605-607.

Rushton, J. P. (1995) *Race, Evolution, and Behavior.* New Brunswick NJ: Transaction.

Scarr, S., & Weinberg, R. A. (1976) IQ test performance of black children adopted by white families. *American Psychologist, 31,* 726-739.

Schuler, G. D., & 103 co-authors. (1996) A gene map of the human genome. *Science, 274,* 540-546.

Shriver, M. D., Smith, M. W., Jin, L., Marcini, A., Akey, J. M., Deka, R., & Ferrell, R. E. (1997) Ethnic-affiliation estimation by use of population-specific DNA markers. *American Journal Human Genetics, 60,* 957-964.

Waldman, I. D., Weinberg, R. A., & Scarr, S. (1994) Racial-group differences in IQ in the Minnesota transracial adoption study: A reply to Levin and Lynn. *Intelligence, 19,* 29-44.

Washburn, S. L. (1978) Human behavior and the behavior of other organisms. *American Psychologist, 33,* 405-418.

Weinberg, R. A., Scarr, S., & Waldman, I. D. (1992) The Minnesota transracial adoption study: A follow-up of IQ test performance at adolescence. *Intelligence, 16,* 117-135.

Whitney, G. (1990) A contextual history of behavior genetics. In: M. E. Hahn, J. K. Hewitt, N. D. Henderson, & R. H. Benno (Eds.), *Developmental Behavior Genetics: Neural, Biometrical, and Evolutionary Approaches.* New York: Oxford University Press. Pp. 7-24.

Whitney, G. (1996) Professor Shockley's experiment. *The Mankind Quarterly, 37,* 41-60.

Whitney, G. (1997) Raymond B. Cattell and the fourth inquisition. *The Mankind Quarterly, 38,* 99-125.

C8✠

CRLEO

Contributors

Michael Hart, "Racial Partition of the United States"

Prof. Hart holds a bachelor's degree in mathematics from Cornell and a Ph.D. in astronomy from Princeton. He also holds advanced degrees in physics, computer science and law. He has worked at NASA Goddard Space Flight Center, Hale Observatories, and the National Center for Atmospheric Research.

Prof. Hart has published a variety of articles in scientific journals and is the author of *The 100: A Ranking of the Most Influential Persons in History*. This book has a world-wide reputation and has been translated into many foreign languages, including Japanese, Chinese, and Arabic. Prof. Hart is also co-editor of *Extraterrestrials: Where Are They?* He taught for several years at Trinity University, in San Antonio, Texas and now teaches astronomy and history of science at Anne Arundel Community College in Maryland.

Address: 1700 Gaffney Court, Crofton, Md. 21114

Samuel Francis, "Equality Unmasked"

Dr. Francis holds a bachelor's degree from Johns Hopkins and a Ph.D. in modern history from the University of North Carolina at Chapel Hill. He has worked as a policy analyst at the Heritage Foundation, and from 1981 to 1986 was a legislative assistant to Senator John East (Republican–North Carolina).

Dr. Francis joined the staff of the *Washington Times* in 1986, where he was editorial writer and staff columnist. In both 1989 and 1990 he received the Distinguished Writing Award for Editorial Writing from the American Society of Newspaper Editors (ANSE) and was twice a finalist for the Scripps Howard Foundation's Walker Stone Prize for editorial writing.

Dr. Francis has published many articles and reviews, most frequently in *Chronicles: A Magazine of American Culture*, for which he writes a monthly column. He is the author of *Power and History: The Political Thought of James Burnham* (1984), *Beautiful Losers: Essays on the Failure of American Conservatism* (1993), and *Revolution From the Middle* (1997).

Dr. Francis publishes a monthly newsletter, the *Samuel Francis Letter*, and his twice-weekly newspaper column is syndicated through Tribune Media Services.

Address: Box 19627, Alexandria, Va. 22320

Michael Levin, "Current Fallacies About Race"

Prof. Levin has a Ph.D. in philosophy from Columbia University and has been a professor of philosophy at City University in New York since 1969. His academic specialties include epistemology and the foundation of set theory. He has written approximately 100 articles in learned journals and is the author of *Metaphysics and the Mind-Body Problem* (1979). Selections from his work appear in dozens of textbooks and anthologies, including many used in English courses.

Prof. Levin is better known to general readers for his critique of feminism, *Feminism and Freedom* (1987), which the *Wall Street Journal* described as "severe, systematic and utterly convincing." His exhaustive study of racial differences, *Why Race Matters,* was published in 1997 by Praeger Publishers. He is under contract with Praeger for another book analyzing some of the fashionable myths about homosexuality.

Prof. Levin's views on race have attracted much attention. He was the subject of a *Penthouse* interview and a cover story in *Insight,* and he is a frequent guest on radio and television programs. Some of the less pleasant consequences of his iconoclasm are described in Samuel Francis' contribution to this volume.

Address: Department of Philosophy, City College, New York, N.Y. 10031

Wayne Lutton, "Immigration, Sovereignty, and Survival of the West"

Dr. Lutton received his Ph.D. in history from Southern Illinois University, and has taught college courses on the history and politics of the United States, Europe, and Latin America. He has written over 200 articles and reviews for such magazines as *Chronicles, National Review*, and *Strategic Review,* and appears frequently on radio and television.

Dr. Lutton is co-author of *The Immigration Time Bomb* (1985, revised edition, 1988) and of *The Immigration Invasion* (1994), and has

contributed chapters to *Immigration–Opposing Viewpoints* (1990) and
Will America Drown? *Immigration and the Third World Population
Explosion* (1993), *The Third World–Opposing Viewpoints* (1995), and
Immigration and the American Identity (1995). He is currently Associate Editor of the *Social Contract*.
Address: The Social Contract, 316½ E. Mitchell Sreet, Petoskey,
Mich. 49770

J. Philippe Rushton, "The American Dilemma in World Perspective"

John Philippe Rushton is a John Simon Guggenheim Fellow and
Professor of Psychology at the University of Western Ontario. He holds
two doctorates from the University of London (Ph.D. and D.Sc.) and
has published nearly 200 scientific articles and six books, including a
best-selling introductory psychology text book. His latest book, *Race,
Evolution, and Behavior*, was published in 1995 by Transaction Publishers. He has been elected to fellowship status in the American Association for the Advancement of Science, the American, British, and
Canadian Psychological Associations, and the Galton Institute.

Although Prof. Rushton began his career believing that inequalities
are caused primarily by the environment, his research on human variation has convinced him of the central role of hereditary factors. This
change of view has come at a high price, as Samuel Francis explains in
this volume.
Address: Department of Psychology, University of Western Ontario, London, Ontario, N6A 5C2 Canada.

Jared Taylor, "Race and Nation"

Samuel Jared Taylor holds an undergraduate degree from Yale and
a master's degree in international economics from *l'Institut d'Etudes
Politiques de Paris*. He is best known for his book, *Paved With Good
Intentions* (1992), which *National Review* called "the most important
book to be published on the subject [of race] in many years." He is also
the editor of *American Renaissance* and president of the New Century
Foundation, which publishes AR and sponsored the conference at
which the papers in this collection were delivered.

Mr. Taylor is also an expert on Japan, where he was born and lived
until age 16. He is the author of *Shadows of the Rising Sun: A Critical*

View of the Japanese Miracle (1983), which the *Wall Street Journal*
called "a delightfully readable account of what makes the Japanese
tick." He has taught Japanese at Harvard Summer School (while still an
undergraduate at Yale), been retained as a consultant by American
companies doing business in Japan, and occasionally serves as a court-
room interpreter for Japanese-speaking witnesses.

Mr. Taylor has written for many newspapers and magazines, and is
author of *The Tyranny of the New and Other Essays* (1992).

Address: Box 527, Oakton, Va. 22124

James Thornton, "A Christian Perspective on the American Dilemma"

Father Thornton is an Orthodox priest under the jurisdiction of the
True Orthodox Church of Greece, of which he is Dean of the American
Exarchate. He is a married priest, and lives with his family in Los An-
geles County, where he serves a parish.

Fr. Thornton holds various theological degrees, including a doctorate in advanced pastoral studies from San Francisco Theological Semi-
nary. He is Senior Editor of *Orthodox Tradition* and is a research associate at the Center for Traditionalist Orthodox Studies in Etna, California.

Fr. Thornton has contributed to a variety of religious publications,
including *Greek Orthodox Theological Review, American Benedictine
Review,* and *Orthodox Path.* He is the author of *Wealth and Poverty in
the Teachings of the Church Fathers* and of *Pitirim Sorokin: Prophet of
Spiritual Renewal.* Fr. Thornton's secular writings include over 100
articles and essays for the *New American,* where he has served as a
contributing editor for six years. He has also written for *Chronicles* and
the *Orange County Register.*

Address: Box 2833, Garden Grove, Cal. 92642

Glayde Whitney, "Diversity in the Human Genome"

Prof. Whitney holds a bachelor's degree with Zoology major, and a
Ph.D. in psychology, both from the University of Minnesota. He served
on active duty with the United States Air Force and was a postdoctoral
fellow at the Institute for Behavioral Genetics, University of Colorado,
before joining the faculty of Florida State University in 1970.

He is now a professor in psychology and member of the graduate program in neuroscience at FSU. A past-president of the Behavior Genetics Association, Prof. Whitney is the recipient of a Claude Pepper Award for research excellence from the National Institute on Deafness and Other Communication Disorders, and the Manheimer Award for career contributions to chemosensory sciences from the Monell Chemical Senses Center.

Prof. Whitney serves on the editorial boards of the scientific journals *Behavior Genetics* and *The Mankind Quarterly*, and is a contributing editor to *American Renaissance*.

Address: Department of Psychology, Florida State University, Tallahassee FL 32306-1270

಼಼ಂ

American Renaissance

The conference at which these talks were delivered was sponsored by *American Renaissance*, a monthly publication of the New Century Foundation. AR, which has been described as "a literate, undecieved journal of race, immigration, and the decline of civility," regularly explores the issues raised in this book. Its writers include many of the speakers.

We invite you to become a subscriber.

. . . . ✂ . . . . . .

Subscriber (Your name will not be given out to anyone.)

Name: _____

Address: _____

Address:_____
Please include 9-digit zip code if possible.

Annual Subscription (12 issues) $24.00. For first-class mail please add $6.00. Canada and overseas, US$30.00. Please make check payable to:

American Renaissance, Box 527, Oakton, VA 22124-0527

Tel: (703) 716-0900   Fax: (703) 716-0932
E-mail:AR@AmRen.com